D0788908

NO   '87

DEMCO

Modern Critical Interpretations

Ursula K. Le Guin's
The Left Hand of Darkness

Modern Critical Interpretations

These and other titles in preparation

Modern Critical Interpretations

Ursula K. Le Guin's
The Left Hand of Darkness

Edited and with an introduction by

Harold Bloom
Sterling Professor of the Humanities
Yale University

Chelsea House Publishers ◇ *1987*

NEW YORK ◇ NEW HAVEN ◇ PHILADELPHIA

©1987 by Chelsea House Publishers, a division
of Chelsea House Educational Communications, Inc.,
  95 Madison Avenue, New York, NY 10016
  345 Whitney Avenue, New Haven, CT 06511
  5014 West Chester Pike, Edgemont, PA 19028

Introduction ©1987 by Harold Bloom

Printed and bound in the United States of America

∞ The paper used in this publication meets the minimum
requirements of the American National Standard for Per-
manence of Paper for Printed Library Materials,
Z39.48-1984.

Library of Congress Cataloging-in-Publication Data
Ursula K. Le Guin's The Left Hand of darkness.

  (Modern critical interpretations)
  Bibliography: p.
  Includes index.
  Contents: Ursula Le Guin's archetypal "Winter journey"
/ David Ketter—World-reduction in Le Guin / Fredric
Jameson—The art of social science-fiction / Donald F.
Theall—[etc.]
  1. Le Guin, Ursula K., 1929-   The left hand
of darkness.   [1. Le Guin, Ursula K., 1929-
  The left hand of darkness.   2. American literature—
History and criticism]   I. Bloom, Harold.   II. Series.
PS3562.E42L435   1987   813'.54   86-29974
ISBN 1-55546-064-X (alk. paper)

Contents

Editor's Note

This book brings together the best criticism available that is devoted to Ursula K. Le Guin's masterpiece, *The Left Hand of Darkness,* arranged here in the chronological order of its original publication. I am grateful to Peter Childers for his aid in researching this volume.

My introduction centers upon the ambisexuality of the planet Winter, which seems a more imaginative condition than our bisexuality. The chronological sequence of criticism begins with David Ketterer's analysis, expressing some reservations that the novel's later critics have sought to answer. Fredric Jameson utilizes his deep knowledge of revolutionary literature in his consideration of *Left Hand* as utopian narrative. Utopian dialectics in Le Guin is also the subject of Donald F. Theall, who finds Ai to be an ambivalent narrator.

Martin Bickman, studying the form/content relation in *Left Hand,* rightly finds it to be very nearly a fusion. A consideration of myth and history in that novel by Jeanne Murray Walker is complemented by Eric S. Rabkin's acute exegesis of the relation between free will and perspectivism in the book. Taoism, a central element in *Left Hand,* is employed by Barbara Brown to help us understand the androgyny of the novel.

Speech-act theory is applied to the story by Victoria Myers, who attempts to explain Genly Ai's communication problems upon the planet Winter. Carol McGuirk concludes this volume with an essay that demonstrates Le Guin's place in humanistic tradition by showing how optimism and humanism mark "the limits of subversion" in *The Left Hand of Darkness*.

Introduction

I

In a recent parable, "She Unnames Them" (*The New Yorker,* 21 January 1985), the best contemporary author of literary fantasy sums up the consequences of Eve's unnaming of the animals that Adam had named:

> None were left now to unname, and yet how close I felt to them when I saw one of them swim or fly or trot or crawl across my way or over my skin, or stalk me in the night, or go along beside me for a while in the day. They seemed far closer than when their names had stood between myself and them like a clear barrier: so close that my fear of them and their fear of me became one same fear. And the attraction that many of us felt, the desire to smell one another's scales or skin or feathers or fur, taste one another's blood or flesh, keep one another warm — that attraction was now all one with the fear, and the hunter could not be told from the hunted, nor the eater from the food.

· This might serve as a coda for all Ursula Kroeber Le Guin's varied works to date. She is essentially a mythological fantasist; the true genre for her characteristic tale is *romance,* and she has a high place in the long American tradition of the romance, a dominant mode among us from Hawthorne down to Pynchon's *The Crying of Lot 49.* Because science fiction is a popular mode, she is named as a science-fiction writer, and a certain defiance in her proudly asserts that the naming is accurate. But no one reading, say Philip K. Dick, as I have been doing after reading Le Guin's discussion of his work in *The Language of the Night,* is likely to associate the prose achievement of Le Guin with that of her acknowledged precursor. She is a fierce defender of the possibilities for science fiction, to the extent of calling Philip K. Dick "our own homegrown Borges" and even of implying that Dick ought not to be compared to Kafka only because Dick is "not an absurdist" and his work "is not (as Kafka's was) autistic."

After reading Dick, one can only murmur that a literary critic is in slight danger of judging Dick to be "our Borges" or of finding Dick in the cosmos of Kafka, the Dante of our century. But Le Guin as critic, loyal to her colleagues who publish in such periodicals as *Fantastic, Galaxy, Amazing, Orbit* and the rest, seems to me not the same writer as the visionary of *The Earthsea Trilogy, The Left Hand of Darkness, The Dispossessed* and *The Beginning Place.* Better than Tolkien, far better than Doris Lessing, Le Guin is the overwhelming contemporary instance of a superbly imaginative creator and major stylist who chose (or was chosen by) "fantasy and science fiction." At her most remarkable, as in what still seems to me her masterpiece, *The Left Hand of Darkness,* she offers a sexual vision that strangely complements Pynchon's *Gravity's Rainbow* and James Merrill's *Changing Light at Sandover.* I can think of only one modern fantasy I prefer to *The Left Hand of Darkness,* and that is David Lindsay's *Voyage to Arcturus* (1920), but Lindsay's uncanny nightmare of a book survives its dreadful writing, while Le Guin seems never to have written a wrong or bad sentence. One has only to quote some of her final sentences to know again her absolute rhetorical authority:

> But he had not brought anything. His hands were empty, as they had always been.
>
> > (*The Dispossessed*)
>
> Gravely she walked beside him up the white streets of Havnor, holding his hand, like a child coming home.
>
> > (*The Tombs of Atuan*)
>
> There is more than one road to the city.
>
> > (*The Beginning Place*)
>
> But the boy, Therem's son, said stammering, "Will you tell us how he died? — Will you tell us about the other worlds out among the stars — the other kinds of men, the other lives?"
>
> > (*The Left Hand of Darkness*)

When her precise, dialectical style — always evocative, sometimes sublime in its restrained pathos — is exquisitely fitted to her powers of invention, as in *The Left Hand of Darkness,* Le Guin achieves a kind of sensibility very nearly unique in contemporary fiction. It is the pure storyteller's sensibility that induces in the reader a state of uncertainty, of *not knowing what comes next*. What Walter Benjamin praised in Leskov is exactly relevant to Le Guin:

> Death is the sanction of everything that the storyteller can tell. He has borrowed his authority from death. . . .
>
> The first true storyteller is, and will continue to be, the teller of fairy tales. Whenever good counsel was at a premium, the fairy tale had it, and where the need was greatest, its aid was nearest. This need was the need created by the myth. The fairy tale tells us of the earliest arrangements that mankind made to shake off the nightmare which the myth had placed upon its chest.

Elsewhere in his essay on Leskov, Benjamin asserts that: "The art of storytelling is reaching its end because the epic side of truth, wisdom, is dying out." One can be skeptical of Benjamin's Marxist judgment that such a waning, if waning it be, is "only a concomitant symptom of the secular productive forces of history." Far more impressively, Benjamin once remarked of Kafka's stories that in them, "narrative art regains the significance it had in the mouth of Scheherazade: to postpone the future." Le Guin's narrative art, though so frequently set in the future, not only borrows its authority from death but also works to postpone the future, works to protect us against myth and its nightmares.

I am aware that this is hardly consonant with the accounts of her narrative purposes that Le Guin gives in the essays of *The Language of the Night*. But Lawrence's adage is perfectly applicable to Le Guin: trust the tale, not the teller, and there is no purer storyteller writing now in English than Le Guin. Her true credo is spoken by one of her uncanniest creations, Faxe the Weaver, master of the Foretelling, to conclude the beautiful chapter, "The Domestication of Hunch," in *The Left Hand of Darkness:*

> "The unknown," said Faxe's soft voice in the forest, "the unforetold, the unproven, that is what life is based on. Ignorance is the ground of thought. Unproof is the ground of action. If it were proven that there is no God there would be no religion. No Handdara, no Yomesh, no hearth gods, nothing. But also if it were proven that there is a God, there would be no religion. . . . Tell me, Genly, what is known? What is sure, predictable, inevitable — the one certain thing you know concerning your future, and mine?"

"That we shall die."

"Yes. There's really only one question that can be answered, Genly, and we already know the answer . . . the only thing that makes life possible is permanent, intolerable uncertainty: not knowing what comes next."

The fine irony, that this is the master Foreteller speaking, is almost irrelevant to Le Guin's profound narrative purpose. She herself is the master of a dialectical narrative mode in which nothing happens without involving its opposite. The shrewdly elliptical title, *The Left Hand of Darkness,* leaves out the crucial substantive in Le Guin's Taoist verse:

> Light is the left hand of darkness
> and darkness the right hand of light.
> Two are one, life and death, lying
> together like lovers in kemmer,
> like hands joined together,
> like the end and the way.

The way is the Tao, exquisitely fused by Le Guin into her essentially Northern mythology. "Kemmer" is the active phase of the cycle of human sexuality on the planet Gethen or Winter, the site of *The Left Hand of Darkness.* Winter vision, even in the books widely separated in substance and tone from her masterpiece, best suits Le Guin's kind of storytelling. Mythology, from her childhood on, seems to have meant Norse rather than classical stories. Like Blake's and Emily Brontë's, her imagination is at home with Odin and Yggdrasil. Yet she alters the cosmos of the Eddas so that it loses some, not all, of its masculine aggressiveness and stoic harshness. Her Taoism, rather than her equivocal Jungianism, has the quiet force that tempers the ferocity of the Northern vision.

II

"Visibility without discrimination, solitude without privacy," is Le Guin's judgment upon the capital of the Shing, who in 4370 A.D. rule what had been the United States, in her novel, *City of Illusions.* In an introduction to *The Left Hand of Darkness,* belatedly added to the book seven years after its publication, Le Guin sharply reminds us that: "I write science fiction, and science fiction isn't about the future. I don't know any more about the future than you do, and very likely less." Like Faxe the Weaver, she prefers ignorance of the future, and yet, again like Faxe, she is a master of

Foretelling, which both is and is not a mode of moral prophecy. It is, in that it offers a moral vision of the present; it is not, precisely because it refuses to say that "If you go on so, the result is so." The United States in 1985 still offers "visibility without discrimination, solitude without privacy." As for the United States in 4370, one can quote "Self," a lyric meditation from Le Guin's rather neglected *Hard Words and Other Poems* (1981):

> You cannot measure the circumference
> but there are centerpoints:
> stones, and a woman washing at a ford,
> the water runs red-brown from what she washes.
> The mouths of caves. The mouths of bells.
> The sky in winter under snowclouds
> to northward, green of jade.
> No star is farther from it than the glint
> of mica in a pebble in the hand,
> or nearer. Distance is my god.

Distance, circumference, the unmeasurable, god, the actual future which can only be our dying; Le Guin evades these, and her narratives instead measure wisdom or the centerpoints. Yet the poem just before "Self" in *Hard Words,* cunningly titled "Amazed," tells us where wisdom is to be found, in the disavowal of "I" by "eye," a not un-Emersonian epiphany:

> The center is not where the center is
> but where I will be when I follow
> the lines of stones that wind about a center
> that is not there
>   but there.
> The lines of stones lead inward, bringing
> the follower to the beginning
> where all I knew
>   is new.
> Stone is stone and more than stone;
> the center opens like an eyelid opening.
> Each rose a maze: the hollow hills:
> I am not I
>   but eye.

One thinks of the shifting centers in every Le Guin narrative, and of her naming the mole as her totem in another poem. She is a maze maker or "shaper of darkness/into ways and hollows," who always likes the country on the other side. Or she is "beginning's daughter" who "sings to stones." Her Taoism celebrates the strength of water over stone, and yet stone is her characteristic trope. As her words are hard, so are most of her women and men, fit after all for Northern or winter myth. One can say of her that she writes a hard-edged phantasmagoria, or that it is the Promethean rather than the narcissistic element in her literary fantasy that provides her with her motive for metaphor.

In some sense, all of her writings call us forth to quest into stony places, where the object of the quest can never quite be located. Her most mature quester, the scientist Shevek in *The Dispossessed,* comes to apprehend that truly he is both subject and object in the quest, always already gone on, always already there. A Promethean anarchist, Shevek has surmounted self-consciousness and self-defense, but at the cost of a considerable loss in significance. He represents Le Guin's ideal Odonian society, where the isolated idealist like Shelley or Kropotkin has become the norm, yet normative anarchism cannot be represented except as permanent revolution, and permanent revolution defies aesthetic as well as political representation. Shevek is beyond these limits of representation and more than that, "his hands were empty, as they had always been." Deprived of the wounded self-regard that our primary narcissism converts into aggression, Shevek becomes nearly as colorless as the actual personality upon whom he is based, the physicist Robert Oppenheimer. Even Le Guin cannot have it both ways; the ideological anarchism of *The Dispossessed* divests her hero of his narcissistic ego, and so of much of his fictive interest. Jung is a better psychological guide in purely mythic realms, like Le Guin's Earthsea, than he is in psychic realms closer to our own, as in *The Dispossessed.*

III

Le Guin's greatest accomplishment, certainly reflecting the finest balance of her powers, is *The Left Hand of Darkness,* though I hasten to name this her finest work to *date.* At fifty-five, she remains beginning's daughter, and there are imaginative felicities in *The Beginning Place* (1980) that are subtler and bolder than anything in *The Left Hand of Darkness* (1969). But conceptually and stylistically, *Left Hand* is the strongest of her dozen or so major narratives. It is a book that sustains many rereadings, partly because its enigmas are unresolvable, and partly because it has the crucial quality of a great representation, which is that it yields up new perspectives upon what we call reality. Though immensely popular (some thirty paperback printings), it seems to me critically undervalued, with rather too much emphasis upon its supposed flaws. The best known negative critique is by Stanislaw Lem, who judged the sexual element in the book irrelevant to its story, and improbably treated in any case. This is clearly a weak misreading on Lem's part. What the protagonist, Genly Ai, continuously fails to understand about the inhabitants of the planet Winter is precisely that their sexuality gives them a mode of consciousness profoundly alien to his (and ours). Le Guin, with admirable irony, replied to feminist and other critics that indeed she had "left out too much" and could "only be very grateful to those readers, men and women, whose willingness to participate in the experiment led them to fill in that omission with the work of their own imagination." Too courteous to say, with Blake, that her care was not to make matters explicit to the idiot, Le Guin wisely has relied upon her extraordinary book to do its work of self-education across the fifteen years of its reception.

The book's principal aesthetic strength is its representation of the character and personality of Estraven, the Prime Minister who sacrifices position, honor, freedom and finally his life in order to hasten the future, by aiding Genly Ai's difficult mission. As the ambassador of the Ekumen, a benign federation of planets, Ai needs to surmount his own perspective as a disinterested cultural anthropologist if he is to understand the androgynes who make up the entire population of the isolated planet alternatively called Gethen or Winter. Without understanding, there is no hope of persuading them, even for their own obvious good, to join with the rest of the cosmos. What is most interesting about Ai (the name suggesting at once the ego, the eye, and an outcry of pain) is his reluctance to go beyond the limits of his own rationality, which would require seeing the causal link between his sexuality and mode of consciousness.

The sexuality of the dwellers upon the planet Winter remains Le Guin's subtlest and most surprising invention:

A Gethenian in first-phase kemmer, if kept alone or with others not in kemmer, remains incapable of coitus. Yet the sexual impulse is tremendously strong in this phase, controlling the entire personality, subjecting all other drives to its imperative. When the individual finds a partner in kemmer, hormonal secretion is further stimulated (most importantly by

touch — secretion? scent?) until in one partner either a male
or female hormonal dominance is established. The genitals engorge or shrink accordingly, foreplay intensifies, and
the partner, triggered by the change, takes on the other sexual role (without exception? If there are exceptions, resulting
in kemmer-partners of the same sex, they are so rare as to be
ignored).

The narrator here is neither Ai nor Le Guin but a field investigator of
the Ekumen, wryly cataloging a weird matter. Her field notes add a
number of sharper observations: these androgynes have no sexual drive
at all for about 21 or 22 out of every 26 days. Anyone can and usually does
bear children, "and the mother of several children may be the father of
several more," descent being reckoned from the mother, known as "the
parent in the flesh." There is no Oedipal ambivalence of children toward
parents, no rape or unwilling sex, no dualistic division of humankind into
active and passive. All Gethenians are natural monists, with no need to
sublimate anything, and little inclination towards warfare.

Neither Le Guin nor any of her narrators gives us a clear sense of
any causal relation between a world of nearly perpetual winter and the
ambisexual nature of its inhabitants, yet an uncanny association between the context of coldness and the unforseeable sexuality of each individual persists throughout. Though Lem insisted anxiety must attend
the unpredictability of one's gender, Le Guin's book persuasively refuses
any such anxiety. There is an imaginative intimation that entering upon
any sexual identity for about one-fifth of the time is more than welcome
to anyone who must battle perpetually just to stay warm! Le Guin's
humor, here as elsewhere, filters in slyly, surprising us in a writer who is
essentially both somber and serene.

The one Gethenian we get to know well is Estraven, certainly a more
sympathetic figure than the slow-to-learn Ai. Estraven is Le Guin's
greatest triumph in characterization, and yet remains enigmatic, as he
must. How are we to understand the psychology of a manwoman, utterly
free of emotional ambivalence, of which the masterpiece after all is the
Oedipal conflict? And how are we to understand a fiercely competitive
person, since the Gethenians are superbly agonistic, who yet lacks any
component of sexual aggressiveness, let alone its cause in a sexually
wounded narcissism? Most fundamentally we are dualists, and perhaps
our involuntary and Universal Freudianism (present even in a professed
Jungian, like Le Guin) is the result of that being the conceptualized

dualism most easily available to us. But the people of Winter are Le Guin's shrewd way of showing us that all our dualisms — Platonic, Pauline, Cartesian, Freudian — not only have a sexual root but are permanent because we are bisexual rather than ambisexual beings. Freud obviously would not have disagreed, and evidently Le Guin is more Freudian than she acknowledges herself to be.

Winter, aside from its properly ghastly weather, is no utopia. Karhide, Estraven's country, is ruled by a clinically mad king, and the rival power, Orgoreyn, is founded upon a barely hidden system of concentration camps. Androgyny is clearly neither a political nor a sexual ideal in *The Left Hand of Darkness*. And yet, mysteriously and beautifully, the book suggests that Winter's ambisexuality is a more imaginative condition than our bisexuality. Like the unfallen Miltonic angels, the Gethenians *know* more than either men or women can know. As with the angels, this does not make them better or wiser, but evidently they *see* more than we do, since each one of them is Tiresias, as it were. This, at last, is the difference between Estraven and Genly Ai. Knowing and seeing more, Estraven is better able to love, and freer therefore to sacrifice than his friend can be.

Yet that, though imaginative, is merely a generic difference. Le Guin's art is to give us also a more individual difference between Ai and Estraven. Ai is a kind of skeptical Horatio who arrives almost too late at a love for Estraven as a kind of ambisexual Hamlet, but who survives, like Horatio, to tell his friend's story:

> For it seemed to me, and I think to him, that it was from that sexual tension between us, admitted now and understood, but not assuaged, that the great and sudden assurance of friendship between us rose: a friendship so much needed by us both in our exile, and already so well proved in the days and nights of our bitter journey, that it might as well be called, now as later, love. But it was from the difference between us, not from the affinities and likenesses, but from the difference, that that love came.

The difference is more than sexual, and so cannot be bridged by sexual love, which Ai and Estraven avoid. It is the difference between Horatio and Hamlet, between the audience's surrogate and the tragic hero, who is beyond both surrogate and audience. Estraven dies in Ai's arms, but uttering his own dead brother's name, that brother having been his incestuous lover, and father of Estraven's son. In a transference both curious and moving, Estraven has associated Ai with his lost brother-lover, to whom he had vowed faithfulness. It is another of Le Guin's strengths that, in context, this has intense pathos and nothing of the grotesque whatsoever. More than disbelief becomes suspended by the narrative art of *The Left Hand of Darkness*.

IV

That Le Guin, more than Tolkien, has raised fantasy into high literature, for our time, seems evident to me because her questers never abandon the world where we have to live, the world of Freud's reality principle. Her praise of Tolkien does not convince me that *The Lord of the Rings* is not tendentious and moralizing, but her generosity does provide an authentic self-description:

> For like all great artists he escapes ideology by being too quick
> for its nets, too complex for its grand simplicities, too fan-
> tastic for its rationality, too real for its generalizations.

This introduction could end there, but I would rather allow Le Guin to speak of herself directly:

> Words are my matter. I have chipped one stone
> for thirty years and still it is not done,
> that image of the thing I cannot see.
> I cannot finish it and set it free,
>
> > transformed to energy.

There is a touch of Yeats here, Le Guin's voice being most her own in narrative prose, but the burden is authentic Le Guin: the sense of limit, the limits of the senses, the granite labor at hard words, and the ongoing image that is her characteristic trope, an unfinished stone. Like her Genly Ai, she is a far-fetcher, to use her own term for visionary metaphor. It was also the Elizabethan rhetorician Puttenham's term for transumption or metalepsis, the trope that reverses time, and makes lateness into an earliness. Le Guin is a grand far-fetcher or transumer of the true tradition of romance we call literary fantasy. No one else now among us matches her at rendering freely "that image of the thing I cannot see."

The Left Hand of Darkness:
Ursula K. Le Guin's Archetypal
"Winter-Journey"

David Ketterer

As distinct from the general recognition that a relationship exists between mythology and any form of literature, science-fiction criticism has recently made much of science fiction as a peculiarly significant vehicle for myth. Unfortunately this idea is being taken rather too literally by a growing number of science-fiction writers, with the result that their work, far from being the articulation of a "new mythology," to use a current critical cliché, consists essentially of the sterile revamping of the old. It is not of course totally erroneous to speak of science fiction as a "new mythology," but what I wish to deplore is the lack of particularity that generally accompanies such assertions. New-mythology critics are curiously loath to offer specific examples, although possible exhibits are certainly at hand. There is for instance what might be called the "terminal beach" myth, to appropriate Ballard's title, the notion being that, just as, in Darwin's view, the transposition of life from the sea to the land allowed for the genesis of humanity, so the end of man might appropriately be envisaged as taking place "on the beach," to utilize Nevil Shute's title. H. G. Wells is perhaps the originator of this "myth." His time traveler's glimpses of Earth's end are from "a sloping beach," while, in a short story entitled "The Star" (1897), the destruction that follows in the wake of that errant body is depicted as follows: "Everywhere the waters were pouring off the land, leaving mud-silted ruins, and the earth littered like a storm-worn beach with all that had floated, and the dead bodies of the men and brutes, its children."

From *New Worlds for Old: The Apocalyptic Imagination, Science Fiction and American Literature.*
©1974 by David Ketterer. Indiana University Press, 1974.

In Northrop Frye's formulation, the mythic basis of any fiction, aside from the occasional reworkings of an O'Neill or a Sartre, should exist irrespective of an author's intentions and in a severely displaced relationship to the story line. In science-fiction novels such as *The Einstein Intersection* (1967) and *Nova* (1968), by Samuel R. Delany, and some of Roger Zelazny's work, there is no doubt as to the author's conscious awareness of his mythic source material and very little attempt at displacement aside from matters of environment. Inevitably in such fictions the logic of plot development is at the service of a mythic structure, and suffers accordingly. *The Left Hand of Darkness,* by Ursula K. Le Guin, the 1969 Hugo *and* Nebula Award winner, is a further case in point. But something is gained here, because, to a degree, this work functions as a science-fiction novel about the writing of a science-fiction novel and is particularly informative for that reason. Since the various fictional genres can be meaningfully defined in relation to basic myths or to segments of myth, the mythic concern of Le Guin's novel, in spite of its attendant deleterious effects on the narrative, does have its point.

As I have argued, science fiction is concerned with effecting what might be termed an epistemological or philosophical apocalypse. A new world destroys an old world. Given that this apocalyptic transformation involves the mythic structure of death and rebirth, for which the cycle of the seasons is the model, we can speculate as to why Gethen, the new world in *The Left Hand of Darkness,* enjoys such an inhospitable climate that the place is known, in English, as Winter. At the same time perhaps we can hypothesize some connection with Frye's "mythos of winter," by which he distinguishes the duplicitous modes of irony and satire, as opposed to the unitary, "apocalyptic" mode of romance. Science fiction draws very much on the combination of satire and romance, and the concepts of unity and duality are, as I shall indicate, central to the theme of Le Guin's book.

II

The Left Hand of Darkness tells a story set in the distant future. Genly Ai has spent two unprofitable years in the nation of Karhide, on the planet Gethen, his mission being to persuade Gethen to join the Ekumen, a loose confederation of eight or so worlds. Because of a political dispute over the desirability of joining the Ekumen and doubt as to its very existence, Ai's Gethenian friend, Estraven, one time senior councilor to Argaven XV, the mad king of Karhide, is exiled and replaced in office by his opponent, Tibe. The king gives Ai the impression that Estraven has been exiled not for promoting the Ekumen's cause, as officially stated, but for working against it.

His faith in Estraven undermined and otherwise generally frustrated, Ai tries his cause elsewhere within the Great Continent, which is divided between Karhide and the rival nation of Orgoreyn, to the northwest. At this point Estraven had already begun his exile, in Orgoreyn. The central portion of the narrative chronicles, in more or less alternating chapters, the respective yet linked careers of Ai and Estraven in Orgoreyn. Ai has the more eventful time. He crosses over at a disputed border area known as the Sinoth Valley, and his first night's sleep in Orgoreyn is interrupted by a raid from Karhide that leaves Ai without his passport (an inspector having kept it for the night) to join a group of refugees from the raid, who, also lacking identification papers, are incarcerated in a windowless cellar. The machinations of Shusgis, First Commensal District Commissioner of Entry-Roads and Ports, extricate Genly from this predicament and bring him to the Commissioner's home in Mishnory, the largest city on Gethen. In Mishnory, Genly runs into Estraven, from whom he learns something of the danger of his situation. Apparently Shusgis is a representative of the Domination faction, which is opposed to the Free Trade faction. In short, Shusgis is opposed to the Envoy's mission, and is actually an agent of the Sarf, a police organization that controls the Free Trade faction. Consequently Genly is imprisoned again, this time at the Pulefen Farm and Resettlement Agency, in the frigid northwest of Orgoreyn.

With the help of Estraven, who has, to a degree, controlled Genly's progress (he plays a part in arranging that Genly feel disposed to leave Karhide when the king begins to favor an unfriendly faction), the Envoy escapes. The concluding third of the book traces their tortuous journey "north through the mountains, east across the Gobrin, and down to the border at Guthen Bay" — the Gobrin being the notorious ice sheet and the border being that fronting on Karhide. Estraven had sent word to King Argaven of the Envoy's arrest on the assumption that Argaven, ignoring Tibe's advice, would inquire and would be falsely informed by Mishnory of Genly's unfortunate death. Estraven later believes that, on discovering Genly's presence in North Karhide, Argaven, now aware of Orgoreyn's duplicitous treatment of the Envoy, would be sympathetic to Genly's mission and enable him to safely call down his star ship, which has all the time been circling Gethen. Except that Estraven, a traitor in his own country, is shot attempting to cross the border back into Orgoreyn, everything, however unlikely, happens as planned: Gethen joins the Ekumen.

III

That an "intelligible" summary of the often arbitrary action of Le Guin's novel is possible without any mention of what it is that makes the Gethenians especially distinctive, especially alien — namely their unique form of bisexuality — argues against the book's structural integrity. The truth of the situation appears to be that Gethenian sexuality, like Gethen's climate, has less to do with the surface plot than with the underlying mythic pattern of destruction or division and creation or unity. Making sense of the novel, and this is its essential weakness, depends upon an act of dislocation on the part of the reader and seeing what should be implicit as explicit, seeing the way in which the mythic structure rigorously, almost mechanically, determines the various turns of the plot. The Gethenians alternate between periods of twenty-one or twenty-two days when they are sexually neuter, neither male nor female, and six-day periods of *kemmer*, when they become sexually active and take on sexual identity. When a Gethenian in kemmer has located a partner in a similar condition, intercourse is possible. During the successive phases of kemmer, one of the parties will develop male sexual organs and the other, female, depending upon how they react to one another. It is therefore possible for any Gethenian to become pregnant. Incest, except between generations, is allowed, with minor restrictions.

It is proposed that, as a result of their ambisexuality, Gethenians are much less prone to the dualistic perception that conceivably is related to the permanent male/female split that characterizes most other forms of humanity: "There is no division of humanity into strong and weak halves, protective/protected, dominant/submissive, owner/chattel, active/passive." Commenting on the Orgota (i.e., of Orgoreyn) word translated as "commensal," "commensality," for almost any form of group organization, Genly remarks on "this curious lack of distinction between the general and specific applications of the word, in the use of it for both the whole and the part, the state and the individual, in this imprecision is its precisest meaning." As one of the Handdarata Foretellers (whom Genly consults at one point), Estraven is "less aware of the gap between men and beasts, being more occupied with the likenesses, the links, the whole of which living things are a part." Genly concludes, "You're isolated, and undivided. Perhaps you are as obsessed with wholeness as we are with dualism."

This Gethenian peculiarity is epitomized by the book's title, which is extracted from "Tormer's Lay":

> Light is the left hand of darkness
> and darkness the right hand of light.

Here is capsulized the destruction of unity and the re-emergence of unity out of a disparate duality, a movement implicit in the thesis-antithesis-synthesis structural arrangement of the book and a movement basic to my theoretical definition of science fiction. From the Gethenian point of view, a unified Gethenian reality is destroyed by the knowledge of the much larger reality of the Ekumen confederation prior to being incorporated in that larger unity. Likewise, the reader's terrestrial vision is destroyed and then reintegrated to the extent that, during the reading process, he accepts the world of Gethen with its aberrant sexuality and the apocalyptic suggestion that both Gethen and Terran civilization were experiments by superior beings on the planet Hain. Le Guin's book effects a philosophical apocalypse in the three ways that science fiction can: by presenting a radically different image of man, by pointing to the existence of a previously unsuspected outside manipulator, and thirdly, as a consequence, by radically altering man's vision of human reality. The sense of mystical unity that "Tormer's Lay" initially suggests suffers an interim disorientation because of the paradoxical equation of the concrete with the abstract and the reversed correlation of light with the left hand, given the sinister associations of left, and of darkness with the right hand. But, almost immediately, the traditional association between the female and the left and between the female and primal darkness helps reintegrate the breach.

IV

The state of division that Genly brings to Gethen is dramatized by means of a series of widening objective correlatives. Estraven, the first alien to whom we are introduced, is presented twice by Genly as "the person on my left," hence somewhat apart and unfamiliar. The king of Karhide, being mad, is presumably divorced from his true self and thus a symbol of disorder and chaos. Hence the efficacy of deception and the rise of Tibe to power, Tibe who is spoken of as possessing the non-Gethenian trick of hate. Of course the major analogy for the state of duality, division, and destruction resides in this piece of information from Estraven: "You know that Karhide and Orgoreyn have a dispute concerning a stretch of our border in the high North Fall near Sassinoth." We are told, "If civilization has an opposite, it is war," with the implication that we infer the opposition between order and chaos. In normal times war is unknown in Gethen, perhaps because of the lack of continuous sexual differentiation. It is hypothesized that war may "be a purely masculine displacement-activity, a vast Rape."

In Orgoreyn both Genly and Estraven are in exile, a condition of separation, Genly from his kind and Estraven from his homeland, although, in some ways, faction-ridden Orgoreyn is a mirror image of Karhide just as Gethen is an inverted image of Earth. As Estraven is approaching the shore of Orgoreyn, he observes, "Darkness lay behind my back, before the boat, and into darkness I must row." For Genly the experience in Orgoreyn is also that of darkness, darkness betokening the destruction of reality, death and chaos. The raid that issues from an unspecified border town of Karhide appears to be a dream. After supper in Siuwensin, Genly "fell asleep in that utter country silence that makes your ears ring. I slept an hour and woke in the grip of a nightmare about explosions, invasions, murder, and conflagration." This is the moment of the apocalypse. Although Genly has mentioned waking, he continues to speak of what is happening as a dream: "It was a particularly bad dream, the kind in which you run down a strange street in the dark with a lot of people who have no faces, while houses go up in flame behind you, and children scream." From this moment until Genly's revival or rebirth from his mock death (arranged by Estraven to aid the escape from Orgoreyn), unreal in a literal sense but real in a symbolic sense, the reader cannot be totally sure that everything is not a dream. But this intervening loss of a stable reality, one of the more subtle aspects of the book, is exactly appropriate as an analogy for the destructive effect the apocalyptic transformations of science fiction have on conventional reality. Thus it is that *The Left Hand of Darkness* may be viewed as a science-fiction novel about the theoretical definition of science fiction.

In his "dream," Genly is incarcerated with a group of refugees in a windowless "vast stone semi-cellar": "The door shut, it was perfectly dark: no light." Genly is metaphorically "in the dark" for most of the time in Orgoreyn, as witness his ambiguous description of Mishnory, the capital city: "It was not built for sunlight. It was built for winter." Yet, at the same time, Genly felt as if he had "come out of a dark age" in Karhide. This sense of unreality is subsequently confirmed by Genly's description of the buildings of central Mishnory: "Their corners were vague, their façades streaked, dewed, smeared. There was something fluid, insubstantial, in the very heaviness of this city built of monoliths, this monolithic state which called the part and the whole by the same name."

Later, confined in a windowless truck on his way to Pulefen Farm, Genly begins to understand the chaotic nature of Orgoreyn:

> It was the second time I had been locked in the dark with un-complaining, unhopeful people of Orogoreyn. I knew now the sign I had been given my first night in this country. I had ignored that black cellar and gone looking for the substance of Orgoreyn above ground, in daylight. No wonder nothing had seemed real.

Genly is suffering the sense of dislocated confusion attendant upon his awareness of a new world — the lack of co-ordinate points: "One's magnetic and directional substances are all wrong on other planets; when the intellect won't or can't compensate for that wrongness, the result is a profound bewilderment, a feeling that everything, literally, has come loose." This is, of course, also a description of the apocalyptic sense of disorientation that the reader of science fiction experiences and that is perhaps the major reason why he reads the stuff. This experience is not unique to science fiction; it is just more purely expressed in the science-fiction form. Indeed the repeated references to the truck as a "steel box," "our box," and "existence in the steel box" are surely reminiscent of Private Henry Fleming's experiences, in a sense apocalyptic, in *The Red Badge of Courage,* as a member of an army that is referred to as a directionless "moving box." And it is surely not accidental that Estraven's first job on arrival in Orgoreyn involves running "a machine which fits together and heatbonds pieces of plastic to form little transparent boxes," symbols presumably of unconscious containment, isolation, alienation, separation, and hence destruction and chaos. As a final analogy to the import of dualism, the mock death of Genly and the deaths of Estraven and of King Argaven's son all betoken the destruction of an old world of mind in the face of a radically new vision.

V

The extent to which the mythic pattern of death and rebirth underlies the action of the novel is reinforced by the "myths" injected into the book in relation to various aspects of the plot. The myth of the

"Place Inside the Blizzard," in which two brothers, one then dead, who had vowed kemmering to one another, are momentarily reunited, bears on the later action. Hode, the dead brother, seized the other, Gethenen, "by the left hand," which, as a consequence, was frozen and subsequently amputated. The Place Inside the Blizzard is clearly a mystic point where life and death may be united. It subsequently transpires that Estraven had vowed kemmering to his now-dead brother although, as Estraven reflects, his "shadow followed me." Later, as anticipated, Estraven and Genly find themselves "inside the blizzard," a kind of still point. This mythic configuration culminates at the novel's conclusion when, Genly is introduced to Sorve Harth, the child of the two brothers, now both dead. Thus life and death are one, on intuition rather clumsily underscored by the book's final lines, Sorve's question to Genly regarding Estraven: "Will you tell us how he died? — Will you tell us about the other worlds out among the stars — the other kinds of men, the other lives?"

Estraven, in fact, has a family history of bringing unity out of discord through "treachery," as is indicated in the Romeo-and-Juliet-like mythic story of "Estaven the Traitor." The matching hands of two mortal enemies make for a reconciliation. This is the myth Estraven re-enacts with Genly. Although they are aliens to each other, they become as one, particularly when Estraven exhibits a capacity for telepathic communication or "bespeaking," as it is appropriately termed. In this way, the mind expansion attendant upon the awareness of a new reality is made both metaphoric and literal. Why speak of telepathic communication as the "Last Art" if not to insinuate the possibility of an apocalypse of mind? And although it is not possible to communicate telepathically anything other than the truth, Estraven believes at one point that it is his dead brother Arek bespeaking him rather than Genly.

Later, as a consequence of this telepathic awareness, Genly, hearing Estraven's words, believes that he himself spoke them. This is a confusion that the reader is made to share, since, although most of the story is told from Genly's point of view, several chapters, without warning, are narrated from Estraven's perspective. Genly explains: "The story is not all mine, nor told by me alone. Indeed I am not sure whose story it is; you can judge better. But it is all one, and if at moments the facts seem to alter with an altered voice, why then you can choose the fact you like best; yet none of them are false, and it is all one story." What confusion exists is designed to augment the impression of unity. There is a similar gain in chapter 7, "The Question of Sex," where Le Guin plays on the reader's expectations by delaying, until the end of the chapter, the revelation that the anthropological notes by Ong Tot Oppong are the work of a woman.

Unity of awareness is also enjoyed by the Handdarata Foretellers, who are introduced in the chapter of injected myth called "The Nineteenth Day," which illustrates the rather vague nature of their prophecies, a vagueness Genly recognizes when he consults them. The Foretellers are controlled by Faxe the Weaver, who brings the various disparate and chaotic forces together like "the suspension-points of a spiderweb." Indeed the weaving imagery, which permeates the book and may be related to the triangular netlike structure created by the relationship of unity to duality, finds its nucleus here. Genly feels himself "hung in the center of a spiderweb woven of silence," "a point or figure in the pattern, in the web." The act of putting together a novel and creating an aesthetic unity can be imagined as a weaving process. Thus Genly speaks of forgetting "how I meant to weave the story." Estraven, making his way to rescue Genly from Pulefen Farm, travels by caravan "weaving from town to town." Traveling between two volcanoes, Drumner and Dremegole, the hissing sound of Drumner, which is in eruption, "fills all the interstices of one's being." These "interstices" may be seen as objectified by the "crevasses" or "crevassed area" to which repeated references are made during the journey across the ice; objectified also by the indirect, crisscross path that Genly and Estraven travel, invariably turning "east-northeast by compass" or "a little south of east" and almost never directly north, south, east, or west. On a larger scale, what is referred to as the "shifgrethor" relationship in Gethenian society appears to be a theoretical network or unformulated pattern of right behavior, rather similar in fact to that web of world known as the Ekumen, which is not so much a "body politic, but a body mystic" modeled on the process of evolution. In view of the importance of webbed relationships to the awareness of a new unity, it is in no way accidental that Faxe the Weaver, at the end of the book, is likely to take Tibe's place as the Prime Minister of Karhide.

VI

The Left Hand of Darkness, which begins with a chapter entitled "A Parade in Erhenrang" and ends with chapters entitled "Homecoming" and "A Fool's Errand," is primarily concerned with the journey from Karhide to Orgoreyn, "One Way" or "Another Way," and back to Karhide following "The Escape" from Pulefen Farm. Physically the journey describes a jagged clockwise circle. I mention its being clockwise because the book, beginning and ending in late spring, covers a temporal cycle. What is being dramatized is the ulitimate unity of space and time. Since Gethen is known as the planet Winter, when Genly speaks of his and Estraven's "winter-journey" it is intended that the reader infer the identification of space and time — it is a journey across and through Winter with, as I have intimated, all the associations of Frye's mythos of winter. The period of death and destruction here symbolized by winter is occasioned by the conjunction of an old and a new world of mind, the basic concern of science fiction.

The journey to and across the ice is replete with imagery suggestive of the forces of creation. Two injections of Gethenian myth point the way. "On Time and Darkness" explains that "Meshe [note the net implications] is the Center of Time," Meshe being the founder of the Yomesh cult, which broke from the Handdarata. Genly experiences something of this insight traveling by truck with a group of prisoners to Pulefen Farm: "We drew together and merged into one entity occupying one space." One member of the group dies. It is significant that just before Estraven's death, Genly is "taken by fits of shuddering like those I had experienced in the prison-truck crossing Orgoreyn." Once again it should be apparent that all the narrative action illustrates the two basic structures of division/duality and unity. The sense of Temporal unity at Meshe is perhaps the inspiration for the Gethenian method of numbering the year backward and forward from the present year, which is consequently always at the center.

"An Orgota Creation Myth" provides a second pointer. We are told, "In the beginning there was nothing but ice and the sun," a notation that explains the landscape through which Genly and Estraven have just passed. The previous chapter ends with a reference to "the veiled sun, the ice." In the process of reaching the blindingly white Gobrin Glacier, white with all the implications of fusion and unity that the color holds for Poe at the polar conclusion of his *Narrative of A. Gordon Pym,* Genly and Estraven have made their way between the two volcanoes of Drumner and Dremegole, Drumner in eruption. The impression is of "the dirty chaos of a world in the process of making itself." The creation myth concludes with a reference to Meshe, "the middle of time," which explains the environment of the next chapter. On the Gobrin Glacier, Genly feels himself and Estraven to be "at the center of all things." It is "On the Ice" that Genly truly comes to recognize Estraven as both man and woman. "Until then I had rejected him, refused him his own reality." The telepathic experience and the experience "Inside the Blizzard" follows his understanding. This mutual understanding, which is equivalent to a rebirth, is symbolized by changes in the environment as "that bland blind nothingness about us began to flow and writhe" and the incident in which Genly "delivers" Estraven from a crevasse into which he falls to emerge with a vision of "Blue — all blue — Towers in the Depths." The crevasses become the cracks in an eggshell, with Genly and Estraven both inside and outside.

This unifying sense of a microcosm and macrocosm is dramatized by the arrival of the Ekumen starship. It is as if the world view of the Ekumen and that of Gethen are collapsed together. Genly plans his call to the ship with a consciousness of setting "the keystone in the arch." One thinks perhaps of Hart Crane's bridge or the bridge on Jupiter in the first volume of Blish's *Cities in Flight* but more particularly of the keystone ceremony with which *The Left Hand of Darkness* opens, which is now seen for its symbolic significance. From among the stars, which have earlier been likened to "far cities," the approaching ship is quite literally "one star descending" I say literally because it represents "the coming of a new world, a new mankind." For the reader, a metaphorical conflation of Earth and Gethen has already taken place encouraged by King Argaven's initially disconcerting reference to Gethenians as "human beings here on earth" and by Estraven's similar reference to Gethen as "this earth." In addition Genly points out, "Fundamentally Terra and Gethen are very much alike. All the inhabited worlds are."

My point has been that Le Guin's use of duality and unity as mythically connotative of destruction and creation is in fact a way of talking about the relationship between new and old worlds of mind and that this relationship is at the theoretical basis of science fiction. As such, *The Left Hand of Darkness* is a skillfully integrated, perhaps I should say woven, piece of work, although my criticism that the plot is unfortunately subordinate to the overly conscious use of mythic material remains. The world of the novel, like the snowbound ecology of Gethen and the snowy metaphors it gives rise to, is developed with a consistency that at least equals Frank Herbert's sandbound world of *Dune*. Mention of "a snow-worm" recalls the sand-worms of *Dune* (1965), which figure so prominently in the plot of that novel. But Le Guin's single and singular reference is perhaps indicative of that loss of dramatic surface incident compelled by her rigorous adherence to a mythic design insufficiently displaced. To use a repeated Gethenian image of unity, the wheel of Le Guin's plot turns rather too inexorably and predictably in its seasonal and mythic groove.

World-Reduction in Le Guin: The Emergence of Utopian Narrative

Fredric Jameson

Huddled forms wrapped in furs, packed snow and sweaty faces, torches by day, a ceremonial trowel and a corner stone swung into place. . . . Such is our entry into the *other* world of *The Left Hand of Darkness* (*LHD*), a world which, like all invented ones, awakens irresistable reminiscences of this the real one—here less Eisenstein's Muscovy, perhaps, than some Eskimo High Middle Ages. Yet this surface exoticism conceals a series of what may be called "generic discontinuities," and the novel can be shown to be constructed from a heterogeneous group of narrative modes artfully superposed and intertwined, thereby constituting a virtual anthology of narrative strands of different kinds. So we find here intermingled: the travel narrative (with anthropological data), the pastiche of myth, the political novel (in the restricted sense of the drama of court intrigue), straight SF (the Hainish colonization, the spaceship in orbit around Gethen's sun), Orwellian dystopia (the imprisonment on the Voluntary Farm and Resettlement Agency), adventure-story (the flight across the glacier), and finally even, perhaps, something like a multi-racial love-story (the drama of communication between the two cultures and species).

Such structural discontinuities, while accounting for the effectiveness of *LHD* by comparison with books that can do only one or two of these things, at once raise the basic question of the novel's ultimate unity. In what follows, I want to make a case for a thematic coherence which has little enough to do with plot as such, but which would seem to

From *Science-Fiction Studies* 2, no. 3 (November 1975).©1975 by SFS Publications.

shed some light on the process of world-construction in fictional narratives in general. Thematically, we may distinguish four different types of material in the novel, the most striking and obvious being that of the hermaphroditic sexuality of the inhabitants of Gethen. The "official" message of the book, however, would seem to be rather different than this, involving a social and historical meditation on the institutions of Karhide and the capacity of that or any other society to mount full-scale organized warfare. After this, we would surely want to mention the peculiar ecology, which, along with the way of life it imposes, make of *LHD* something like an anti-*Dune;* and, finally, the myths and religious practices of the planet, which give the book its title.

The question is now whether we can find something that all these themes have in common, or better still, whether we can isolate some essential structural *homology* between them. To begin with the climate of Gethen (known to the Ekumen as Winter), the first Investigator supplies an initial interpretation of it in terms of the resistance of this ice-age environment to human life:

> The weather of Winter is so relentless, so near the limit of tolerability even to them with all their cold-adaptations, that perhaps they use up their fighting spirit fighting the cold. The marginal peoples, the races that just get by, are rarely the warriors. And in the end, the dominant factor in Gethenian life is not sex or any other human being: it is their environment, their cold world. Here man has a crueler enemy even than himself.
>
> (CHAP. 7)

However, this is not the only connotation that extreme cold may have; the *motif* may have some other, deeper, disguised symbolic meaning that can perhaps best be illustrated by the related symbolism of the tropics in recent SF, particularly in the novels of J.G. Ballard. Heat is here conveyed as a kind of dissolution of the body into the outside world, a loss of that clean separation from clothes and external objects that gives you your autonomy and allows you to move about freely, a sense of increasing contamination and stickiness in the contact between your physical organism and the surfaces around it, the wet air in which it bathes, the fronds that slap against it. So it is that the jungle itself, with its non- or anti-Wordsworthian nature, is felt to be some immense and alien organism into which our bodies run the risk of being absorbed, the most alarming expression of this anxiety in SF being perhaps that terrible scene in Silverberg's *Downward to Earth* (chap. 8) in which the protagonist discovers a human couple who have become hosts to some unknown parasitic larvae that stir inside thier still living torso like monstrous foetuses.

This loss of physical autonomy — dramatized by the total environment of the jungle into which the European dissolves — is then understood as a figure for the loss of psychic autonomy, of shich the utter demoralization, the colonial whisky-drinking and general dissolution of the tropical hero is the canonical symbol in literature. (Even more relevant to the present study is the relationship between extreme heat and sexual anxiety — a theme particularly visible in the non-SF treatments of similar material by Catholic novelists like Graham Greene and Francois Mauriac, for whom the identification of heat and adolescent sexual torment provides ample motivation for the subsequent desexulization experienced by the main characters.)

Ballard's work is suggestive in the way in which he translates both physical and moral dissolution into the great ideological myth of entropy, in which the historic collapse of the British Empire is projected outwards into some immense cosmic deceleration of the universe itself as well as of its molecular building block. This kind of ideological message makes it hard to escape the feeling that the heat symbolism in question here is a peculiarly Western and ethnocentric one. Witness, if proof be needed, Vonnegut's *Cat's Cradle,* where the systematic displacement ot the action from Upstate New York to the Caribbean, from dehumanized American scientists to the joyous and skeptical religious practices of Bokononism, suggests a scarecely disuised meditation on the relationship between American power and the Third World, between repression and scientific knowledge in the capitalist world, and a nostalgic and primitivistic evocation of the more genuine human possibilities available in an older and simpler culture. The preoccupation with heat, the fear of sweating as of some dissolution of our very being, would then be tantamount to an unconscious anxiety about tropical field-labor (an analogous cultural symbolism can be found in the historical echo of Northern factory work in the blue jeans and work-shirts of our own affluent society). The nigthmare of the tropics thus expresses a disguised terror at the inconceivable and unformulable threat posed by the masses of the Third World to our own prosperity and privilege, and suggests a new and unexpected framework in which to interpret the icy climate of Le Guin's Gethen.

In such a reading the cold weather of the planet Winter must be understood, first and foremost, not so much as a rude environment, in-hospitable to human life, as rather a symbolic affirmation of the autonomy of the organism, and a fantasy realization of some virtually total disengagement of the body from its environment or eco-system. Cold *isolates,* and the cold of Gethen is what brings home to the characters (and the reader) their physical detachment, their free-standing isolation as separate individuals, goose-flesh transforming the skin itself into some outer envelope, the sub-zero temperatures of the planet forcing the organism back on its own inner resources and making of each a kind of self-sufficient blast-furnace. Gethen thus stands as an attempt to imagine an experimental landscape in which our being-in-the-world is simplified to the extreme, and in which our sensory links with the multiple and shifting perceptual fields around us are abstracted so radically as to vouchsafe, perhaps, some new glimpse as to the ultimate nature of human reality.

It seems to me important to insist on this cognitive and experimental function of the narrative in order to distinguish it from other, more night-marish representations of the sealing off of consciousness from the external world (as e.g., in the "half-life" of the dead in Philip K. Dick's *Ubik*). One of the most significant potentialities of SF as a form is precisely this capacity to provide something like an experimental variation on our own empirical universe; and Le Guin has herself described her invention of Gethenian sexuality along the lines of just such a "thought experiment" in the tradition of the great physicists: "Einstein shoots a light-ray through a moving elevator; Schrödinger puts a cat in a box. There is no elevator, no cat, no box. The experiment is performed, the question is asked, in the mind." Only one would like to recall that "high literature" once also affirmed such aims. As antiquated as Zola's notions of heredity and as naive as his fascination with Claude Bernard's account of experimental research may have been, the naturalist concept of the *experimental novel* amounted, on the eve of the emergence of modernism, to just such a reassertion of literature's cognitive function. That his assertion no longer seems believable merely suggests that our own particular environment—the total system of late monopoly capital and of the consumer society—feels so massively in place and its reification so overwhelming and impene-trable, that the serious artist is no longer free to tinker with it or to project experimental variations. The historical opportunities of SF as a literary form are intimately related to this paralysis of so-called high literature. The officially "non-serious" or pulp character of SF is an indispensable feature in its capacity to relax that tyrannical "reality principle" which functions as a crippling censorship over high art, and to allow the "para-literary" form thereby to inherit the vocation of giving us alternate versions of a world that has elsewhere seemed to resist even *imagined* change. (This account of the transfer of one of the most vital traditional functions of literature to SF would seem to be confirmed by the increasing efforts of present-day "art literature"—e.g., Thomas Pynchon— to reincorporate those formal capacities back into the literary novel.)

The principal techniques of such narrative experimentation—of the systematic variation, by SF, of the empirical and historical world around us—have been most conveniently codified under the twin headings of *analogy* and *extrapolation.* The reading we have proposed of Le Guin's experimental ecology suggests, however, the existence of yet a third and quite distinct technique of variation which it will be the task of the remainder of this analysis to describe. It would certainly be possible to see the Gethenian environment as extrapolating one of our own Earth seasons, in an extrapolation developed according to its own inner logic and pushed to its ultimate conclusions—as, for example, when Pohl and Kornbluth project out onto a planetary scale, in *The Space Merchants,* huckstering trends already becoming visible in the nascent consumer society of 1952; or when Brunner, in *The Sheep Look Up,* catastrophically speeds up the environment pollution already underway. Yet this strikes me as being the least interesting thing about Le Guin's experiment, which is based on a principle of systematic exclusion, a kind of surgical excision of empirical reality, something like a process of ontological attenuation in which the sheer teeming multiplicity of what exists, of what we call reality, is deliberately thinned and weeded out through an operation of radical abstraction and simplification which we will henceforth term *world-reduction.* And once we grasp the nature of this technique, its effects in the other thematic areas of the novel become inescapable, as for instance in the conspicuous absence of other animal species on Gethen. The omission of a whole grid-work of evolutionary phyla can, of course, be accounted for by the hypothesis that the colonization of Gethen, and the anomalous sexuality of its inhabitants, were the result of some forgotten biological experiment by the original Hainish civilization, but it does not make that lack any less disquieting: "There are no communal insects on Winter. Gethenians do not share their earth as Terrans do with those older societies, those innumerable cities of little sexless workers possessing no instinct but that of obedience to the group, the whole" (chap. 13).

But it is in Le Guin's later novel, *The Dispossessed (TD)* that this situation is pushed to its ultimate consequences, providing the spectacle of a planet (Anarres) in which human life is virtually without biological partners:

> It's a queer situation, biologically speaking. We Anarresti are unnaturally isolated. On the old World there are eighteen phyla of land animal; there are classes, like the insects, that have so many species they've never been able to count them, and some of these species have populations of billions. Think of it: everywhere you looked animals, other creatures, sharing the earth and air with you. You'd feel so much more a *part.*
>
> (CHAP. 6)

Hence Shevek's astonishment, when on his arrival in Urras, he is observed by a face "not like any human face . . . as long as his arm, and ghastly white. Breath jetted in vapor from what must be nostrils, and terrible, unmistakable, there was an eye" (chap. 1). Yet the absence, from the Anarres of *TD,* of large animals such as the donkey which here startles Shevek, is the negative obverse of a far more positive omission, namely that of the Darwinian life-cycle itself, with its predators and victims alike: it is the sign that human beings have surmounted historical determinism, and have been left alone with themselves, to invent their own destinies. In *TD,* then, the principle of world-reduction has become an instrument in the conscious elaboration of a utopia. On Gethen, however, its effects remain more tragic, and the Hainish experiment has resulted in the unwitting evolution of test-tube subjects rather than in some great and self-conscious social laboratory of revolution and collective self-determination:

> Your race is appallingly alone in its world. No other mammalian species. No other ambisexual species. No animal intelligent enough even to domesticate as pets. It must color your thinking, this uniqueness . . . to be so solitary, in so hostile a world: it must affect your entire outlook.
>
> (CHAP. 16)

Still, the deeper import of such details, and of the constructional principle at work in them, will become clear only after we observe similar patterns in other thematic areas of the novel, as, for instance, in Gethenian religion. In keeping with the book's antithetical composition, to the two principal national units, Karhide and Orgoreyn, correspond two appropriately antithetical religious cults: the Orgota one of Meshe being something like a heresy or offshoot of the original Karhidish Handdara in much the same way that Christianity was the issue of Judaism. Meshe's religion of total knowledge reflects the mystical experience from which it sprang and in which all of time and history became blindingly co-present: the emphasis on knowing, however, suggests a positivistic bias which is as appropriate to the commercial society of Orgoreyn, one would think, as was Protestantism to the nascent capitalism of western Europe. It is, however, the other religion, that of Karhide, which is most relevant to our present argument: the Handdara is, in antithesis to the later sect, precisely a mystique of darkness, a cult of non-knowledge parallel to the drastic reductionism of the Gethenian climate. The aim of its spiritual practice is to strip the mind of its non-essentials and to reduce it to some quintessentially simplified function:

> The Handdara discipline of Presence . . . is a kind of trance — the Handdarate, given to negatives, call it an untrance — involving self-loss (self-augmentation?) through extreme sensual receptiveness and awareness. Though the technique is the exact opposite of most techniques of mysticism it probably is a mystical discipline, tending towards the experience of Immanence.
>
> (CHAP. 5)

Thus the fundamental purpose of the ritual practice of the foretelling — dramatized in one of the most remarkable chapters of the novel — is, by answering *answerable* questions about the future, "to exhibit the perfect uselessness of knowing the answer to the wrong question" (chap. 5), and indeed, ultimately, of the activity of asking questions in general. What the real meaning of these wrong or unanswerable questions may be, we will try to say later on; but this mystical valorization of ignorance is certainly quite different from the brash commercial curiosity with which the Envoy is so pleasantly surprised on his arrival in Orgoreyn (chap. 10).

Now we must test our hypothesis about the basic constructional principle of *LHD* against that picture of an ambisexual species — indeed, an ambisexual *society* — which is its most striking and original feature. The obvious defamiliarization with which such a picture confronts the *lecteur moyen sensuel* is not exactly that of the permissive and counter-cultural tradition of male SF writing, as in Farmer or Sturgeon. Rather than a stand in favor of a wider tolerance for all kinds of sexual behaviour, it seems more appropriate to insist [as does Le Guin herself in her article

"Is Gender Necessary?" In *Aurora: Beyond Equality,* eds. Susan J. Anderson and Vonda McIntyre] on the feminist dimension of her novel, and on its demystification of the sex roles themselves. The basic point about Gethenian sexuality is that the sex role does not color everything else in life, as is the case with us, but is rather contained and defused, reduced to that brief period of the monthly cycle when, as with our animal species, the Gethenians are in "heat" or "kemmer." So the first Investigator sent by the Ekumen underscores this basic "estrangement-effect" of Gethen on "normally" sexed beings:

> The First Mobile, if one is sent, must be warned that unless he is very self-assured, or senile, his pride will suffer. A man wants his virility regarded, a woman wants her femininity appreciated, however indirect and subtle the indications of regard and appreciation. On Winter they will not exist. One is respected and judged only as a human being. It is an appalling experience.
>
> (CHAP. 7)

That there are difficulties in such a representation (e.g., the unavoidable designation of gender by English pronouns), the author is frank to admit in the article referred to. Still, the reader's failures are not all her own, and the inveterate tendency of students to describe the Gethenians as "sexless" says something about the limits imposed by stereotypes of gender on their own imaginations. Far from eliminating sex, indeed, Gethenian biology has the result of eliminating sexual *repression:*

> Being so strictly defined and limited by nature, the sexual urge of Gethenians is really not much interferred with by society: there is less coding, channeling, and repressing of sex than in any bisexual society I know of. Abstinence is entirely voluntary; indulgence is entirely acceptable. Sexual fear and sexual frustration are both extremely rare.
>
> (CHAP. 13)

The author was in fact most careful not merely to *say* that these people are not eunuchs, but also — in a particularly terrifying episode, that of the penal farm with its anti-kemmer drugs — to *show* by contrast what eunuchs in this society would look like (chap. 13).

Indeed, the vision of public kemmer-houses (along with the sexual license of utopia in *TD*) ought to earn the enthusiasm of the most hardcore Fourierist or sexual libertarian. If it does not quite do that, it is because there is another, rather different sense in which my students were not wrong to react as they did and in which we meet, once again, the phenomenon we have called world-reduction. For if Le Guin's Gethen does not do away with sex, it may be suggested that it does away with everything that is *problematical* about it. Essentially, Gethenian physiology *solves* the problem of sex, and that is surely something no human being of our type has ever been able to do (owing largely to the nonbiological nature of human desire as opposed to "natural" or instinctual animal need). Desire is permanently scandalous precisely because it admits of no "solution" — promiscuity, repression, or the couple all being equally intolerable. Only a makeup of the Gethenian type, with its limitation of desire to a few days of the monthly cycle, could possibly curb the problem. Such a makeup suggests that sexual desire is something that can be completely removed from other human activities, allowing us to see them in some more fundamental, unmixed fashion. Here again, then, in the construction of this particular projection of desire which is Gethenian ambisexuality, we find a process at work, which is structurally analogous to that operation of world-reduction or ontological attenuation we have described above: the experimental production of an imaginary situation by *excision* of the real, by a radical suppression of features of human sexuality which cannot but carry a powerful fantasy-investment in its own right. The dream of some scarcely imaginable freedom from sex, indeed, is a very ancient human fantasy, almost as powerful in its own way as the outright sexual wish-fulfillments themselves. What its more general meaning in *LHD* might be, we can only discover by grasping its relationship to that other major theme of the novel which is the nature of Gethenian social systems, and in particular, their respective capacities to wage war.

It would seem on first glance that the parallelism here is obvious and that, on this particular level, the object of what we have been calling world-reduction can only be institutional warfare itself, which has not yet developed in Karhide's feudal system. Certainly Le Guin's work as a whole is strongly pacifistic, and her novella "The Word for World is Forest" is (along with Aldiss' *Dark Light-Years*) one of the major SF denunciations of the American genocide in Vietnam. Yet it remains an ethical, rather than a socioeconomic, vision of imperialism, and its last line extends the guilt of violence to even that war of national liberation of which it has just shown the triumph: "'Maybe after I die people will be as they were before I was born, and before you came. But I do not think so'" (chap. 8). Yet if there is no righteous violence, then the long afternoon and twilight of Earth will turn out to be just that onerous dystopia

SF writers have always expected it would.

This properly liberal, rather than radical, position in Le Guin seems to be underscored by her predilection for quietistic heroes and her valorization of an anti-political, anti-activist stance, whether it be in the religion of Karhide, the peaceable traditions of the "creechies," or in Shevek's own reflective temperament. What makes her position more ambiguous and more interesting, however, is that Le Guin's works reject the institutionalization of violence rather than violence itself: nothing is more shocking in *TD* than the scene in which Shevek is beaten into unconsciousness by a man who is irritated by the similarity between their names:

> "You're one of those little profiteers who goes to school to keep his hands clean," the man said. "I've always wanted to knock the shit out of one of you." "Don't call me profiteer!" Shevek said, but this wasn't a verbal battle. Shevet knocked him double. He got in several return blows, having long arms and more temper than his opponent expected: but he was outmatched. Several people paused to watch, saw that it was a fair fight but not an interesting one, and went on. They were neither offended nor attracted by simple violence. Shevek did not call for help, so it was nobody's business but his own. When he came to he way lying on his back on the dark ground between two tents.
>
> (CHAP. 2)

Utopia is, in other words not a place in which humanity is freed from violence, but rather one in which it is released from the multiple determinisms (economic, political, social) of history itself: in which it settles its accounts with its ancient collective fatalisms, precisely in order to be free to do whatever it wants with its interpersonal relationships — whether for violence, love, hate, sex or whatever. All of that is raw and strong, and goes farther towards authenticating Le Guin's vision — as a return to fundamentals rather than some beautification of existence — than any of the explanations of economic and social organization which *TD* provides.

What looks like conventional liberalism in Le Guin (and is of course still ideologically dubious to the very degree that it continues to "look like" liberalism) is in reality itself a use of the Jeffersonian and Thoreauvian tradition against important political features of that imperializing liberalism which is the dominant ideology of the United States today — as her one contemporary novel, *The Lathe of Heaven,*

makes plain. This is surely the meaning of the temperamental opposition between the Tao-like passivity of Orr and the obsession of Haber
with apparently reforming and ameliorative projects of all kinds:

> The quality of the will to power is, precisely, growth. Achieve-
> ment is its cancellation. To be, the will to power must increase
> with each fulfillment, making the fulfillment only a step to a
> further one. The vaster the power gained, the vaster the ap-
> petite for more. As there was no visible limit to the power
> Haber wielded through Orr's dreams, so there was no end to
> his determination to improve the world.
>
> (CHAP. 9)

The pacifist bias of *LHD* is thus part of a more general refusal of the
growth-oriented power dynamics of present-day American liberalism,
even where the correlations it suggests between institutionalized warfare,
centralization, and psychic aggression may strike us a preoccupations of a
characteristically liberal type.

I would suggest, however, that beneath this official theme of warfare, there are details scattered here and there throughout the novel
which suggest the presence of some more fundamental attempt to
reimagine history. What reader has not indeed been struck—without
perhaps quite knowing why—by descriptions such as that of the opening
cornerstone ceremony: "Masons below have set an electric winch going,
and as the king mounts higher the keystone of the arch goes up past him
in its sling, is raised, settled, and fitted almost soundlessly, great ton-
weight block though it is, into the gap between the two piers, making
them one, one thing, an arch" (chap. 1); or of the departure of the first
spring caravan towards the fastnesses of the North: "twenty bulky,
quiet-running, barge-like trucks on caterpillar treads, going single file
down the deep streets of Erhenrang through the shadows of morning"
(chap. 5)? Of course, the concept of *extrapolation* in SF means nothing if it
does not designate just such details as these, in which heterogenous or
contradictory elements of the empirical real world are juxtaposed and
recombined into piquant montages. Here the premise is clearly that of a
feudal or medieval culture that knows electricity and machine technology. However, the machines do not have the same results as in our
own world: "The mechanical-industrial Age of Invention in Karhide is
at least three thousand years old, and during those thirty centuries they
have developed excellent and economical central-heating devices using
steam, electricity, and other principles; but they do not install them in

their houses" (chap. 3). What makes all this more complicated than the usual extrapolative projection is, it seems to me, the immense time span involved, and the great antiquity of Karhide's science and technology, which tends to emphasize not so much what happens when we thus combine or amalgamate different historical stages of our own empirical Earth history, but rather precisely *what does not happen*. That is, indeed, what is most significant about the example of Karhide, namely that *nothing* happens, an immemorial social order remains exactly as it was, and the introduction of electrical power fails — quite unaccountably and astonishingly to us — to make any impact whatsoever on the stability of a basically static, unhistorical society.

Now there is surely room for debate as to the role of science and technology in the evolution of the so-called West (i.e., the capitalist countries of western Europe and North America). For Marxists, science developed as a result both of technological needs and of the quantifying thought-modes inherent in the emergent market system; while an anti-Marxist historiography stresses the fundamental role played by technology and inventions in what now becomes strategically known as the Industrial Revolution (rather than capitalism). Such a dispute would in any case be inconceivable were not technology and capitalism so inextricably intertwined in our own history. What Le Guin has done in her projection of Karhide is to sunder the two in peremptory and dramatic fashion:

> Along in those four millennia the electric engine was developed, radios and power looms and power vehicles and farm machinery and all the rest began to be used, and a Machine Age got going, gradually, without any industrial revolution, without any revolution at all.
>
> (CHAP. 2)

What is this to say but that Karhide is an attempt to imagine something like a West which would never have known capitalism? The existence of modern technology in the midst of an essentially feudal order is the sign of this imaginative operation as well as the gauge by which its success can be measured: the miraculous presence, among all those furs and feudal *shifgrethor,* of this emblematically quiet, peacefully humming technology is the proof that in Karhide we have to do not with one more specimen of feudal SF, but rather precisely with an alternate world to our own, one in which — by what strange quirk of fate? — capitalism never happened.

It becomes difficult to escape the conclusion that this attempt to rethink Western history without capitalism is of a piece, structurally and in its general spirit, with the attempt to imagine human biology without desire which we have described above; for it is essentially the inner dynamic of the market system which introduces into the chronicle-like and seasonal, cyclical, tempo of pre-capitalist societies the fever and ferment of what we used to call *progress*. The underlying identification between sex as an intolerable, wellnigh gratuitous complication of exist-ence, and capitalism as a disease of change and meaningless evolutionary momentum, is thus powerfully underscored by the very technique — that of world-reduction — whose mission is the utopian exclusion of both phenomena.

Karhide is, of course, not a utopia, and *LHD* is not in that sense a genuinely utopian work. Indeed, it is now clear that the earlier novel served as something like a proving ground for techniques that are not consciously employed in the construction of a utopia until *TD*. It is in the latter novel that the device of world-reduction becomes transformed into a sociopolitical hypothesis about the inseparability of utopia and scarcity. The Odonian colonization of barren Anarres offers thus the most thoroughgoing literary application of the technique, at the same time that it constitutes a powerful and timely rebuke to present-day at-tempts to parlay American abundance and consumers' goods into some ultimate vision of the "great society."

I would not want to suggest that all of the great historical utopias have been constructed around the imaginative operation which we have called world-reduction. It seems possible, indeed, that it is the massive commodity environment of late capitalism that has called up this par-ticular literary and imaginative strategy, which would then amount to a political stance as well. So in William Morris's *News from Nowhere,* the hero — a nineteenth-century visitor to the future — is astonished to watch the lineaments of nature reappear beneath the fading inscription of the grim industrial metropolis, the old names on the river themselves transfigured from dreary slang into the evocation of meadow land-scapes, the slopes and streams, so long stifled beneath the pavements of tenement buildings and channeled into sewage gutters, now reemergent in the light of day:

> London, which — which I have read about as the modern Babylon of civilization, seems to have disappeared. . . . As to the big murky places which were once, as we know, the

centres of manufacture, they have, like the brick and mortar desert of London, disappeared; only, since they were centres of nothing but "manufacture," and served no purpose but that of the gambling market, they have left less signs of their existence than London. . . . On the contrary, there has been but little clearance, though much rebuilding, in the smaller towns. Their suburbs, indeed, when they had any, have melted away into the general country, and space and elbow-room has been got in their centres; but there are the towns still with their streets and squares and market-places; so that it is by means of these smaller towns that we of today can get some kind of idea of what the towns of the older world were alike, — I mean to say, at their best.

Morris's utopia is, then, the very prototype of an aesthetically and libidinally oriented social vision, as opposed to the technological and engineering-oriented type of Bellamy's *Looking Backward*—a vision thus in the line of Fourier rather than Saint Simon, and more prophetic of the values of the New Left rather than those of Soviet centralism, a vision in which we find this same process of weeding out the immense waste-and-junk landscape of capitalism and an artisanal gratification in the systematic excision of masses of buildings from a clogged urban geography. Does such an imaginative projection imply and support a militant political stance? Certainly it did so in Morris's case; but the issue in our time is that of the militancy of ecological politics generally. I would be inclined to suggest that such "no-places" offer little more than a breathing space, a momentary relief from the overwhelming presence of late capitalism. Their idyllic, yet elegiac, sweetness, their pastel tones, the rather pathetic withdrawal they offer from grimier Victorian realities, seems most aptly characterized by Morris's subtitle to *News from Nowhere*: "*An Epoch of Rest.*" It is as though — after the immense struggle to free yourself, even in imagination, from the infection of our very minds and values and habits by an omnipresent consumer capitalism — on emerging suddenly and against all expectation into a narrative space radically other, uncontaminated by all those properties of the old lives and the old preoccupations, the spirit could only lie there gasping in the fresh silence, too weak, too *new*, to do more than gaze wanly about it at a world remade.

Something of the fascination of *LHD*—as well as the ambiguity of its ultimate message — surely derives from the subterranean within it towards a utopian "rest" of this kind, towards some ultimate "no-place" of a collectivity untormented by sex or history, by cultural superfluities or an object-world irrelevant to human life. Yet we must not conclude without observing that in this respect the novel includes its own critique as well.

It is indeed a tribute to the rigor with which the framework has been imagined that history has no sooner, within it, been dispelled, than it sets fatally in again; that Karhide, projected as a social order without development, begins to develop with the onset of the narrative itself. This is, it seems to me, the ultimate meaning of that *motif* of right and wrong questions mentioned above and resumed as follows: "to learn which questions are unanswerable, and *not to answer them:* this skill is most needful in times of stress and darkness." It is no accident that this maxim follows hard upon another, far more practical discussion about politics and historical problems:

> To be sure, if you turn your back on Mishnory and walk away from it, you are still on the Mishnory road. . . . You must go somewhere else; you must have another goal; then you walk a different road. Yegey in the Hall of the Thirty-Three today: 'I unalterably oppose this blockade of grain-exports to Karhide, and the spirit of competition which motivates it.' Right enough, but he will not get off the Mishnory road going that way. He must offer an alternative. Orgoreyn and Karhide both must stop following the road they're on, in either direction; they must go somewhere else, and break the circle.
>
> (CHAP. 11)

But, of course, the real alternative to this dilemma, the only conceivable way of breaking out of that vicious circle which is the option between feudalism and capitalism, is a quite different one from the liberal "solution"—the Ekumen as a kind of galactic United Nations—offered by the writer and her heroes. One is tempted to wonder whether the strategy of *not* asking questions ("Mankind," according to Marx, "always [taking] up only such problems as it can solve") is not the way in which the utopian imagination protects itself against a fatal return to just those historical contradictions from which it was supposed to provide relief. In that case, the deepest subject of Le Guin's *LHD* would not be utopia as such, but rather our own incapacity to conceive it in the first place. In this way too, it would be a proving ground for *TD*.

The Art of Social-Science Fiction: The Ambiguous Utopian Dialectics of Ursula K. Le Guin

Donald F. Theall

THE OUTSIDE OBSERVER IN UTOPIA

The twentieth century has seen the growth of the social sciences and the "humane sciences" as one of its more important developments in speculative thought, a fact increasingly reflected in the concepts of writers of SF, including utopian fiction. Although concern with social and cultural questions has always been a central feature of the utopian tradition within SF, a conscious use of concepts from the social sciences has been considerably slower to develop in SF than that of concepts from the natural sciences. In this development toward artistic self-consciousness the writings of Ursula K. Le Guin occupy a significant role; they are constantly concerned with questions of cultural interaction, cultural growth, communication, and the differences between fictional but always parabolic "highly intelligent life forms."

Le Guin's interest in humane sciences and cultural change appears to be linked to her concern with utopianism. Most of her imaginary societies are models critical of our present societies. Although her first major novel, *The Left Hand of Darkness* (*LHD*), did not, strictly speaking, provide a utopian model, both the nations of Karhide and Orgoreyn are meant as criticisms of the present social and cultural order: the former by contraries, in terms of its anarchistic directions and the latter directly, in terms of its bureaucratization. Further, the broader background of the interplanetary organization of the Ekumen is an "ideal" model with

From *Science-Fiction Studies* 2, no. 3 (November 1975). ©1975 by SFS Publications.

implicit criticisms of contemporary intercommunication between nations. Thus, following the utopian tradition, Le Guin provides a tension between the here-and-now and her various fictional futures. But her fictional future worlds also differ sharply from each other, allowing her to further investigate the potential of various social and cultural developments. Such juxtapositions of fictional societies are a feature of all of her Hainish novels; her only non-Hainish SF novel, *The Lathe of Heaven*, is a psychological study of dreams which materialize, providing a variety of modes of life within the same culture. In her most recent novel, *The Dispossessed: An Ambiguous Utopia* (*TD*), Le Guin overtly juxtaposes the capitalist aggressive and competitive nations on the world of Urras and the anarchist satellite world of Anarres. These two worlds are juxtaposed within the broader framework of an interstellar community of planets containing a possible future world of Earth (Terra), and using the Terran ambassador as a choral commentator on the concluding action of the novel. This counterpoints the entire action of the novel with the here and now, so that Anarres and Urras assume a variety of complex relationships with societies of the present.

Such a strategy of utopian fiction begins with More's juxtaposition of books 1 and 2 in *Utopia* as well as his counterpointing of Utopia as a whole with events in his own historical time. It continues through Swift, who developed it with greater compositional complexity (though not necessarily greater conceptual complexity) in *Gulliver's Travels*. This strategy involves a dialectical logic and an implicit critique of society as well as providing critical rather than futurological models of possible alternative ways of life. In order to achieve this end, Le Guin seems to have quite consciously developed some aspects of this utopian tradition (down to Thoreau and Morris), and in particular the role of *the stranger visiting a new world*. The actual sensory experience and subjective response of strangers or outsiders plays a central role in validating the carefully chosen and believable details which compose the thorough accounts Le Guin gives us of her fictional worlds. In *Rocannon's World* the hero is a museumologist who comes to the planet as a cultural investigator; in *Planet of Exile* both Jakob and Rolery are outsiders who cease to be total strangers in each other's culture; in *City of Illusions* the outsider is a total stranger to the world and unaware, for most of the novel, of his own identity. In each case the separateness of the outsider makes him an observer as well as a participant, and allows for the particularly descriptive approach. In *LHD*, interestingly enough, the stranger — who is also the main narrator — is a professional cultural analyst and cultural communicator, whose concern with a thorough account of the culture provides the novel with the characteristic features of an anthropological report. Yet even in this respect Le Guin employs the techniques of ambivalence, for her field-worker, her "mobile" from the Ekumen to the Gethenians, realizes that the "truth" of the humane sciences is founded in imagination as well as fact:

> I'll make my report as if I told a story, for I was taught as a child on my homeworld that Truth is a matter of imagination. The soundest fact may fail or prevail in the style of its telling; like that singular organic jewel of our seas, which grows brighter as one woman wears it, and worn by another, dulls and goes to dust.
>
> (CHAP. 1)

Le Guin weaves into the utopian social-science fiction the vigorous story-telling techniques used in adventure fantasy. This respect for an imaginative approach means among other things that Genly Ai's subjective emotions become part of his account, permitting others to judge it in the light of his subjective bias. In the telling, the subjective reactions of Ai (the name obviously involves a complex pun on "I," "eye," etc.) are illustrated: reactions to the coldness of the climate, to the sexual problems posed by a world where everyone is a neuter except during periods of *kemmer* when they can become either male or female, to the political anarchy created by a world where there are no worlds and the entire planet is, like Karhide, "a family quarrel" (chap. 1). Le Guin consequently can use Ai as an ambivalent focus, in the same way that Hythloday or Gulliver are used: Ai himself reveals some of the naivete which complicates the action of the novel and impedes the success of his mission. The subjective mode of telling is extended in *TD* to a technique where the third-person narrative reappears, but always with a sense that the action is being seen through the eyes and the feelings of Shevek. Like Ai, Shevek becomes an ambivalent narrator, although like Ai he grows in the process so that his insights by the end of the novel are more perceptive than those at the beginning. Even though Shevek is not the "professional" which Ai is, the work itself develops the fictional societies on Urras and Anarres with the same detail and thoroughness as was done in *LHD*. That is, we learn about the details of physical geography, sexual customs, cultural evolution, ideology, life-style, and the like on the two worlds. The relating of Shevek's learning process, while it includes a fairly thorough anthropological description of the societies in question, involves equally an account of the emotions of Shevek as he explains his experiences.

That Le Guin's overall conception is utopian is apparent in the history and nature of the Ekumen. In our world, where there has been a constant need and desire for a world federation of nations, Le Guin's Ekumen — the most utopian concept of *LHD* — acts as a critique of the everyday strivings in this direction. However, she manages to preserve a dialectical tension which also provides internal criticism of the Ekumen itself. The critique of the Ekumen that is part of the action of *LHD* is part of that idea itself, because the way in which the Ekumen encounters new worlds is to open up a communication or trade of idea in which processes of mutual change take place — just as the First Mobile, Ai, is changed through his contact with Estraven and with the Foretellers as the action unfolds. Thus, Le Guin has a very complex and sophisticated dialectical conception of utopia: the observing outsider is a visual and emotional "eye" that negates its "outside" character by the very process of observing. The tradition of Hythloday and Gulliver is reconstructed in a period highly self-conscious of the humane sciences. Therefore, Le Guin's works and the observers themselves show a high consciousness of these sciences.

LE GUIN AND THE HUMANE SCIENCES:
COMMUNICATION, EDUCATION, AND SOCIAL CRITIQUE

To establish the degree of Le Guin's awareness of the humane sciences it is necessary to explore some of her main themes. These involve among other things: communications, intercultural interaction, social structure, role-playing, ideologies. The prime theme of her major novels and, in fact, the unifying theme of her Hainish novels, is *communication*, particularly communication between different kinds of highly intelligent life forms ("hilfs"). In many ways *LHD* provides a basic pattern for these concerns. Therefore, let us consider here the focus of communication in its action. First of all, Ai's particular mission, which gives rise to the action of the novel, is an attempt on the part of the association of planets, known as the Ekumen, to open communication with new areas where there are intelligent life forms. In performing his function, Ai is fully aware of the difficulties involved in the process of intercultural contact and the need for caution and prudence in the pursuit of intercultural exchange of knowledge. As he points out, the Ekumen send only one envoy (First Mobile) on the first contact with any new planet:

The first voice, one man present in the flesh, present and
alone. He may be killed . . . or locked up with madmen . . .
yet the practice is kept, because it works. One voice speaking
truth is a greater force than fleets and armies, given time;
plenty of time; but time is the thing that the Ekumen has
plenty of.

(CHAP. 3)

He is preceded by a team of undercover investigators, some of whose
reports are cited during the telling of his story; forty years after they
leave, the First Mobile comes. He leaves his ship in space so that it is not
observed, and comes only with his interstellar communication device
(the ansible) and some pictures of his homeworld, so as not to intrude
alien artifacts prematurely into the culture. The Stability of Ekumen has
established a carefully rationalized method of interculture contact and
communication. Exploring the deepest meaning of such communication
becomes one of the central concerns of the novel.

The most relevant differences between Gethen and Ai's homeworld
are the facts that each person can assume the role of either sex in sexual
and parental relations, and that Gethen itself is at the very limit of coldness inhabitable by intelligent life. These facts pose two major problems
for Ai, and provide the novel with some of its major metaphors. The
communication between Ai and the hero of the action, Estraven—
who saves Ai's life and opens Gethen up to the Ekumen—only comes
about through a long and difficult process of understanding. Early on in
his account, Ai suggests that sex or "biological shock" is perhaps the chief
problem, in a world where he can say of the person he rents his quarters
from: "He was so feminine in looks and manner that I once asked how
many children he had. He looked glum. He had never borne any. He
had, however, sired four" (chap. 5). Eventually, after a long period of
isolated companionship while fleeing across a great glacier, Ai comes to
recognize how gender had been an impediment to communication with
Estraven and how, sharing a constant threat of death, he has learned to
overcome this and love Estraven. Speaking of his new awareness of
Estraven gained while crossing the glacier, Ai says:

And I saw then again, and for good, what I had always been
afraid to see, and had pretended not to see in him: that he was
a woman as well as a man. Any need to explain the sources of
that fear vanished with the fear; what I was left with was, at
last, acceptance of him as he was. Until then I had rejected

> him, refused him his own reality. . . . I had not been willing
> to give my trust, my friendship, to a man who was a woman,
> a woman who was a man.
>
> (CHAP. 18)

The unrecognized biological shock has been an impediment to human communication; but once recognized, it provides Ai with a whole new relationship to the culture with which he must work. A symbolic support for the episode is provided by its setting on the glacier. The glacier is a world somewhat like Poe's world in the closing of *Narrative of A. Gordon Pym,* for it is a world of which Estraven says, "There is nothing, the Ice says, but Ice" (chap. 16). The quality of whiteness on this ice world is reminiscent of the one in the writings of Poe and Melville, who would appear to be part of an American tradition of writing to which Le Guin's work is related.

The incident on the ice illustrates Ai's coming to master the genuine art of communication with a Gethenian as a fellow human being, achieving mutual trust and understanding. This justifies the Ekumen's sending a single Mobile to first encounter a new society, as a means of having him learn to establish genuine relations with its inhabitants. Again and again Ai's perceptions, which shift from naivete to understanding as his account unfolds, focus on means of communicating with the society and of understanding the way of education and communication within the society itself. His investigation of the quasi-religious phenomenon of "foretelling," which is so central to Gethenian society, is just such a process, for he comes to realize that the Foretellers are using their understanding of the world in a peculiarly paradoxical way as a means of educating their fellow-Karhidians. The purpose of Foretelling is ultimately not to provide answers but to demonstrate that there is only one question that can be answered—"That we shall die." Therefore, as Faxe says, the basis of foretelling is "the unknown, . . . the unforetold, the unproven, that is what life is based on. Ignorance is the ground of thought. Unproof is the ground of action" (chap. 5). Foretelling within the social structure of Karhide is a basic education in the values of the society. The Foretellers really teach that change cannot be brought about through the reading of prophecies or predictions; that uncertainty is of the essence of the social fabric. The process of Foretelling is a social dramatization of this fact, in that it provides correct answers which are not necessarily (in fact, not usually) helpful answers since they do not cover enough of the future contingencies.

The Ekumen has produced its own form of wisdom for learning the wisdom of others as well as communicating whatever wisdom it may also contain. As Ai attempts to tell the Commensals of Orgoreyn (the bureaucratic collectivist society of Tethen):

> The Ekumen is not essentially a government at all. It is an attempt to reunify the mystical with the political, and as such is of course mostly a failure; but its failure has done more good for humanity so far than the successes of its predecessors. It is a society and it has, at least potentially, a culture. It is a form of education; in one aspect it's a sort of very large school — very large indeed. The motives of communication and cooperation are of its essence.
>
> (CHAP. 10)

The Ekumen as an instrument of education is an instrument of communication, a way towards interplanetary wisdom. Such an approach, however — as Ai realizes and stresses — is essentially a dualistic approach, a fact dramatized in the structures that Le Guin chooses to create in her tales. In a section of Estraven's journal, the following exchange is recounted:

> Ai brooded, and after some time he said, "You're isolated, and undivided. Perhaps you are as obsessed with wholeness as we are with dualism."
>
> "We are dualists too. Duality is an essential, isn't it? So long as there is *myself* and *the other*."
>
> "I and Thou," he said. "Yes, it does, after all, go even wider than sex."
>
> (CHAP. 16)

This duality of "myself and the other" or "I and Thou" is naturally at the heart of human communication, but it is also a duality which generates all of the other dualities in the processes of cognition and understanding. Such a sense of duality is common to all of Le Guin's writings, culminating in the duality of the opposed worlds of *TD*.

The very structure of her works is determined by this theme, for it is a structure of dualities — in *LHD,* of Gethen and the Ekumen, of Karhide and Orgoreyn, of Ai and Estraven. From the bringing together of the dualities and from the understanding that is generated by coming to terms with each of them, the process of discovery by which the meaning of the Ekumen is encompassed comes about. The process is dialectical and complexly critical, for each of the dual ingredients which will end up in creating a wholeness modifies and is modified by the other. Orgoreyn's bureaucracy displays both its greater rationality and its greater tendency towards totalitarianism when viewed against the anarchy and decentralized government of Karhide; Orgoreyn and Karhide show their provincialism in contrast to the Ekumen, but also some of the wisdom gained in having to come to terms more slowly — e.g., without an Industrial Revolution — on the world of Gethen. Finally, because of Le Guin's social-science consciousness, the presence of the contemporary world is to be found in the critical conception of *LHD*. The "simplicity" of Karhide becomes one mode of criticizing many contemporary phenomena; the centralization of Orgoreyn, another. Orgoreyn's prison camps, secret police forces, interminable politics, and incredible bureaucracy are modes of satirizing similar phenomena in our own culture. Karhide's Foretellers with their stress on ignorance become one mode of critical parable directed against the futurologists and the planners. All of Karhide with its different sexual arrangements and the relative peace which is maintained through them becomes a mode of critique of the over-use of sexual stimuli (see particularly chap. 7 of *LHD*).

Le Guin, speaking of *LHD,* has suggested that she does use her novels to explore situations which have their parallel in the real world. She designed the world of Gethen in part to explore the male-female problem in a context where it would be possible to examine the thoughts and feelings of individuals who could be both men and women. But *LHD* goes further, involving a large number of social and human issues as all her novels do. They are utopian in the specific sense of creating some relative perfection as a contrast with the world of the reader.

AMBIGUOUS UTOPIANISM: LE GUIN'S DIALECTICS OF SOCIALIST DEMOCRATIC HUMANISM

For this reason, it is not surprising that Le Guin's most recent, major novel, *TD,* was subtitled "An Ambiguous Utopia." The subtitle calls attention to ambivalence as an overt aspect of much of her work. In *LHD,* the nations of Gethen, in the act of intercultural contact with the Ekumen, also give rise to ambivalence; for example, many of the customs of Karhide, as Ai notes, have much to suggest by way of improvement to a Terran member of the Ekumen. But further, Le Guin uses the essential ambivalence to the utopian tradition. Beginning with More, many possible alternative fictional worlds were conceived as ambivalent, founded in the paradoxes generated by the juxtaposition of fictional models and real worlds. The fondness for paranomasia (puns) in More and Swift reflects this complex ambivalence by which they seduce the uncritical rationalist into double binds. An example which parallels Le Guin's treatment of Anarres occurs when "More" (the fictional character in *Utopia* who has listened to Hythloday's account, including the part about the use of gold and ornament in Utopia — an account paralleling the incident of the necklace in *TD* (chap. 10) remarks on the many values of Utopia but notes that among other qualities the virtue of magnificence — the ethical art of doing and making things well and in the grand manner — is absent from the commonweal. In the context of the narrative, More's (the author's) other works, and the values More saw in the play impulse, this creates precisely such an ambiguous tension; for the necessary critique which the Utopians have performed by suppressing such magnificence will eventually become a problem for them as their society evolves. Part of the tension of More's *Utopia* arises through a double historical vision: Hythloday's awareness — e.g., of the potential for change his own coming to Utopia represents — is more limited than that of "More" (the character) and, of course, More the author. Hythloday's Platonic Utopia is a static concept, though his intrusion into its society — like Ai's intrusion into Gethen — creates a process of historical change. The very nature of the collision between the processes of history and of utopianizing creates an ambiguity, which so many critics attempt to resolve in utopian novels in order to have a definite outcome.

Le Guin, though, is too aware of the tension in the tradition and the fact that it arises out of the process of estrangement which is bound to occur in intercultural communication; the Ekumen as a utopian conception is — as I argued in section 1 — one way of taking this into account. The action of *TD*, therefore, begins before the utopian Ekumen has come into being, so that it explores the problem of utopia within a pre-Ekumenian, relatively pre-utopian framework, so to speak. The parameters within which it does this, though, are the same parameters of "social-science fiction" which mark all of Le Guin's other SF novels.

In *TD*, therefore — as in *LHD* — communication is a central theme and motivation for producing the action of the novel. Intercultural contact again plays a major role and — though not as central to the novel as Ai — a Terran plays the role of chorus at its conclusion when Shevek is given sanctuary in the Terran embassy to Urras. The action of *TD* rises out of its central character's, Shevek's, growing realization that the presumably anarchistic utopian world of Anarres is seriously flawed in many ways, especially in terms of the freedom of communication in ideas. Metaphorically, the world of Anarres as a whole looms more and more like a prison (of which there are none on Anarres)—a metaphor the understanding of which goes back to a childhood experience of Shevek's when he and some of his schoolmates tried to recreate what prison was like on a world that does not have any. The metaphor of prison becomes even more closely linked to inhibition of communication when related to the dominant symbol of the novel—walls. The novel opens with a reference to walls:

> There was a wall. It did not look important. It was built of un-cut rocks roughly mortared. An adult could look right over it, and even a child could climb it. Where it crossed the roadway instead of having a gate it degenerated into mere geometry, a line, an idea of a boundary. But the idea was real. It was important. For seven generations there had been nothing in the world more important than the wall.
>
> Like all walls it was ambiguous, two-faced. What was inside it and what was outside it depended on which side of it you were on.
>
> (CHAP. 1)

The wall could be seen either as enclosing the universe and "leaving Anarres, outside, free" or it could be seen an enclosing Anarres and making it a "great prison camp, cut off from other worlds and other man, in quarantine" (chap. 1).

One dimension of Anarres as an ambiguous utopia—and one that it shares with More's Utopia—is the necessity of cutting itself off from other men and other history. It can maintain its utopian purity only as long as it does not communicate with those outside itself, so that it becomes a total institution. This also means that within the individual groups of "syndicates" that form the anarchistic society there is a substantial control of ideas, a fact Shevek suffers from since his theories of time cannot be developed as he wishes, yet "it is of the nature of an idea to be communicated: written, spoken, done. The idea is like grass. It craves light, like crowds, thrives on cross-breeding, grows better for being stepped on" (chap. 3). As Shevek grows and develops, he becomes dedicated to the liberation of ideas and of the mind; before leaving for Urras, he establishes a printing syndicate on Anarres to communicate ideas which were being inhibited. He finally decides to leave Urras in order "to go fulfill my proper function as a social organism. I'm going to unbuild walls" (chap. 10).

TD begins with Shevek leaving Anarres for Urras, and his earlier life is presented through a series of flashbacks juxtaposed with his current life on Urras, a technique which has obvious affinities with his own Theory of Time. This strategy creates a constant tension between the values of the two worlds and their varying impacts on Shevek. It is one of the clearest devices for demonstrating the weaknesses (and hence ambiguities) in Anarres by exposing it to the one type of scrutiny which it forbids itself from doing. The tension is neither simple nor solely paradoxical, for in Shevek's intensely critical perspective on injustice, poverty, commercialism and other aspects of Urras, and in his final return to Anarres, the novel is achieving a sophisticated reshaping of the world of Anarres within Shevek's vision of what it might be or ought to be. During their meeting, when Keng, the Terran, provides him with sanctuary, she takes exception to Shevek's view that "Hell is Urras." In comparison to the (future) Earth, ecologically destroyed and inhabitable only by means of "total centralization . . . total rationing, birth control, euthanasia, universal conscription into the labour force," Urras seems

> the kindliest, most various, most beautiful of all the inhabited worlds. It is the world that came as close as any could to paradise. I know it's full of evils, full of human injustice, greed, folly, waste. But it is also full of good, of beauty, of vitality, achievement. It is what a world should be! It is *alive*, tremendously alive — alive despite all its evils, with hope.
>
> (CHAP. 11)

This newly introduced perspective performs a function similar to the removing of Karhide and Orgoreyn from the perspective of Gethen to that of the universe, though it is, again, not the final word on Urras, merely a testimony to the hope it still contains.

This complexity of perspectives which Le Guin develops is a characteristic of her works as a whole. *Rocannon's World, Planet of Exile,* and *City of Illusions* all strive for similar conceptual complexities by involving life on worlds with a variety of different peoples inhabiting them and the intrusion of outsiders into these worlds; the tendency in each is towards some ambiguity or ambivalence. In each case, too, the presence of history (a fictional world history) is an important ingredient of the works as well as a constantly implied comparison with the present. But only in *TD* is this overtly linked with a fully articulated theory of time and history which is an intrinsic part of the novel, since it is because of inhibitions to developing and disseminating this theory that Shevek travels from Anarres to Urras and back.

The theory of time propounded by Shevek dialectically interrelates a theory of sequence with a theory of simultaneity. As his social education matures throughout the novel, he comes to apply his theory to social and ethical questions. This suggests to him that — while he left Anarres for Urras because Anarres attempted to sever its communications with history and its past, with those who still lived in it on Urras — Urras as well as the Terran ambassador sever themselves from the future which Anarres presents to them. While Shevek's return to Anarres clearly indicates his preference for his home-world, he returns as a more critical and aware person to await the time when finally the Terrans or the Urrasti will seek out Anarres, ready to understand its values. There's no attempt in the fictional situation to eliminate the ambivalences in Anarres, for they are there partly as a result of a total sociopolitical situation — the Odonian flight from Urras. On the other hand, the story — just as Shevek's theory of history — does not eliminate the possibility of change or hope. In fact, contingency, chance, change are the factors which make Shevek's dream possible. He can begin to develop his unified field theory because he has finally accepted the fact that "In the region of the unprovable, or even the disprovable, lay the only chance for breaking out of the circle and going ahead" (chap. 9). This, too, he discovers in history, the history of his subject — physics. There he learns that the ancient Terran physicist, "Ainsetain," in his unwillingness to accept the indeterminacy principle (in a way similar to the principles of the Karhidians and their Foretellers), had created flaws and inadequacies in his theory, but that the theory is still "as beautiful, as valid, and as useful as ever, after these centuries, and yet both depended upon a hypothesis that could not be proved true and that could be and had been proved false in certain circumstances" (chap. 9).

This, though, demonstrates a greater affinity between art and science; Shevek had discovered that through the fate of his friend Turin, whose imagination could not be contained within the world of Anarres. Le Guin, here, as in her other works, attracts the reader with an ambiguous kind of anarchist or — more generally — subservice dialectic, which has strong roots in the everyday situations of human living and in a sense of history. As in Ai's account, imagination becomes central to the Truth of this critique. The world of contemporary Marxism, the world of contemporary capitalism, the Third World, and the variety of contemporary attitudes towards these, play through each of her novels — including *The Lathe of Heaven* which breaks the normal pattern of historically-oriented works to investigate one founded in the world where dreams create possible future histories. Her dialectic uses the utopian ideas of social science and Marx as a counterpoint to imaginative speculations at every level of her works, from composition and setting to ideas and character. In *TD,* for example, the characters form a world of oppositions through whose communication the mutual education of all develops. Shevek is a physicist, his wife Takver a biologist. Her awareness provides the critique of physical science necessary to come to terms with humanity. Tirin, as the artist, poses the challenge of creativity and of imagination to Shevek; Bedap, the propagandist-philosopher, shows the value of social awareness and social communication. While all of these characters are linked by the bonds of love and friendship, they differ enough so that they can interact, teach and learn from each other. Tirin, for example, "could never build walls. . . . He was a natural rebel. He was a natural Odonian — a real one" (chap. 19). Yet Tirin was not a "strong person." The value of Tirin in the story is that he brings Shevek to see the necessity of unbuilding walls.

Le Guin's treatment of character by means of contrast and opposition parallels her way of dealing with ideas and structures in terms of both balance and imbalance. While balance is obviously a central feature of her writing, she also takes the concept of ambivalence very seriously, stressing history as perpetually upsetting the balance and creating new tensions. Le Guin sees balance as a dynamic principle mediating between oppositions. Hence her preoccupation with the paradox of communication: in order to communicate, it is necessary to recognize differences and to move toward an understanding of these differences. The stress on uncertainty and the recognition of "flaws" — becomes explicit in Shevek's theory — create a sharpened reinterpretation of the Taoist concept of balance in *LHD,* where she had expressed it by way of paradoxical epigram, e.g.: "Darkness is in the mortal eye that thinks it sees and sees not" (chap. 12). Le Guin is in some ways similar to a socialist humanist such as the Polish philosopher Leszek Kolakowski, who in the essay "In Praise of Inconsistency" pointed out that an acceptance of contradiction did not automatically result in a simple balance based on a reconciliation of opposites:

Inconsistency is simply a refusal once and for all to choose beforehand between any values whatever which mutually

exclude each other. A clear awareness of the eternal and in-
curable antinomy in the world of values is nothing but conscious inconsistency, though inconsistency is more often
practiced than proclaimed.

(Leszek Kolakowski, *Toward a Marxist Humanism*)

Kolakowski — who shares Shevek's fate of an exile from a "closed"
society — suggests that inconsistency which is an "awareness of the contradictions in this world" is "a consciously sustained reserve of uncertainty." With Le Guin as with Shevek, the uncertainty is an important
aspect of the balance, for wholeness is only gained in a process of change
and the process of change is only raised to consciousness through her
ambiguous utopian dialectic.

Le Guin's *The Left Hand of Darkness:* Form and Content

Martin Bickman

One of the most effective aspects of Ursula Le Guin's writing is the way "form" and "content" make a seamless whole for which these distinctions can be used only to demonstrate their ultimate unity. This form-content inter-relationship, of course, should be evident in any fine work of literature, but science-fiction writers have traditionally had difficulty in this area. Masters like Clarke, Asimov, Herbert can tell a story skillfully, but seldom see the possibilities of literary form beyond those of direct narrative. On the other hand, SF "experimentalists" in style such as, at various times, Harlan Ellison, Brian Aldiss, John Brunner have been so concerned with "technique" that the results are sometimes more audacious than successful. This article will use *The Left Hand of Darkness* to suggest some of the ways form and content can be wedded in SF in a functional, organic, and aesthetically meaningful way.

The very opening not only shows the book explicitly concerned with this issue, but also gives us clues as to the specific structures used and the underlying rationales.

> I'll make my report as if I told a story, for I was taught as a child on my homeworld that Truth is a matter of the imagination. The soundest fact may fail or prevail in the style of its telling: like that singular organic jewel of our seas, which grows brighter as one woman wears it and, worn by another, dulls and goes to dust. Facts are no more solid, coherent, round, and real than

From *Science-Fiction Studies* 4, no. 1 (March 1977). ©1977 by SFS Publications.

pearls are. But both are sensitive.

The story is not all mine, nor told by me alone. Indeed I am not sure whose story it is; you can judge better. But it is all one, and if at moments the facts seem to alter with an altered voice, why then you can choose the fact you like best; yet none of them are false, and it is all one story.

(CHAP. 1)

Most immediately, the opening suggests that Genly Ai is the structuring consciousness of the book, that his "story" is not only those sections he tells in his own person, but the selection and ordering of everything that appears. That Genly includes Therem's narrative in the latter's own words, that Genly places legends, myths, tales, field notes as they were actually told or written, instead of hammering them into his own single-perspective, linear narrative reflects the "I-Thou" understanding he achieves through the experiences related in the novel. That Genly is in an immediate way the architect of the entire book is implied in his comments about altered voices, and his recognition that, although he cannot say *whose* story it is, he knows that it is all *one* story. This notion is further corroborated by apparently off-hand comments such as "He [Therem] lay in the tent writing, in a little notebook, in his small, rapid, vertical-cursive Karhidish hand, the account that appears as the previous chapter" (chap. 15). The book can be read, in the words of a writer on *symbolisme,* as "the imaginative graph of the experience of the artist lived in the course of his journey to knowledge." Or, more accurately, since this is a novel, not a lyric poem, as a kind of *bildungsroman,* where we share in the central character's process of growth.

As with much modern literature, then, the complex patterning of the book is not so much a way to tell a story as it is the story itself. The opening paragraphs suggest the main lines of this patterning: apparent dualities are placed in a harmonious, complementary relationship without collapsing important distinctions between them. Facts, like pearls, do have an independent existence, are themselves "solid," "round," "real," yet the extent to which they penetrate the consciousness depends on their presentation and context. Similarly, the novel achieves unity not in spite of, but because of its variety of voices and perspectives — different angles of vision that create a certain dimensionality and heft. More generally, the two paragraphs suggest the interweaving pairs of tensions that shape the book: the relationship between the fact and imagination, the literal and the figurative, and that between the one and the many, unity and diversity.

Since few people are either absolute monists or absolute pluralists, the problem is to find a workable relationship between the extremes and the structure of the book grapples with this problem as it appears in the interrelated levels of individual psychology, social and political organization, and religious and philosophical ideas. In the first third we see Karhide moving from a precarious balance between oneness and divisiveness towards a state of mobilization, a premature and ultimately spurious kind of unification. This movement sweeps us into the Orgo-reyn section, where a similar unification has been taking place for centuries, revealing more clearly its effects on the people and culture. In the final third, Genly and Therem create a relationship where the balance between unity and diversity is established on a basis more solid and vital than that depicted at the beginning of the book. Thus, in respect to the unity-diversity tension, the structure of the book follows a dynamic movement that can be viewed roughly as thesis-antithesis-synthesis. Counterpointing this movement is the alternating rhythm of "reality" and "myth," a movement examined later in this paper.

The opening scene, the parade in Karhide, where nobody marches in step, images that country's social and political structure. "The various banners of the great Domains tangle in a rain-beaten confusion of color with the yellow pennants that bedeck the way, and the various musics of each group clash and interweave in many rhythms echoing in the deep, stone street." The contrast of the "tangle" and "confusion" of the variegated flags of the domains with the ordered, single-color pennants that mark out the parade route suggests, along with the phrase "clash and interweave," the balance between the cohesive and the dispersive, a balance clearly tilted at this point toward the latter. Even the Royal Music, the theme of the one man who rules over all this, is a nerve-shaking discord, a "preposterous, disconsolate bellow." The scene prepares us for Therem's aphorism at parade's end: "Karhide is not a nation but a family quarrel" (chap. 1). Genly himself later elaborates: "The principalities, towns, villages, 'pseudo-feudal tribal economic units,' a sprawl and splatter of vigorous, competent, quarrelsome individualities over which a grid of authority was insecurely and lightly laid" (chap. 8). This structure, or lack of it, is only part of an entire cultural configuration shaped by the primary religion of Karhide, the Handdara, "a religion without institution, without priests, without hierarchy, without vows, without creed."

After spending some time at a Handdara retreat, Genly comes to realize the forceful presence of this elusive, impalpable religion, a realization underscored later by his discovery that the former prime minister is a Handdara adept: "Under the nation's politics and parades runs an old darkness, passive, anarchic, silent, the fecund darkness of the Handdara" (chap. 5).

Rather than actually breaking into anarchy, however, Karhide succumbs to a demagogue who would "unite" the country by creating the fear and hatred of the Other that some call patriotism. Although this mobilization seems to run counter to Karhide's basic disposition, one cannot help wondering if the very passivity and formlessness of the culture helps Tibe succeed. Further, if we view the political shift in terms of Gethenian androgynous psychology, we can see that an overemphasis on qualities we might consider "feminine" may bring about a reaction or overcompensation in the direction of "masculine" qualities. As Le Guin writes in a restrospective article on the book:

> To me the "female principle" is, or at least historically has been, basically anarchic. It values order without constraint, rule by custom not by force. It has been the male who enforces the order, who constructs power-structures, who makes, enforces, and breaks laws. On Gethen, these two principles are in balance: the decentralising against the centralising, the flexible against the rigid, the circular against the linear. But balance is a precarious state, and at the moment of the novel the balance, which had leaned towards the "feminine," is tipping the other way.
>
> ("Is Gender Necessary?" in *Aurora: Beyond Equality*,
> eds. Susan J. Anderson and Vonda McIntyre)

As Genly, who is described in the same article as a "conventional, indeed rather stuffy young man," moves into Orgoreyn, he is pleased by what he experiences as a welcome change from the earlier Karhide: "There was no clutter and contortion, no sense of always being under the shadow of something high and gloomy, as in Erhenrang; everything was simple, grandly conceived, and orderly. I felt as if I had come out of a dark age, and wished I had not wasted two years in Karhide" (chap. 8). But if the earlier Karhide is a little too fragmented, shadowy, diverse, Orgoreyn leans much further and more dangerously in the other direction. Uniqueness and individuality are sacrificed to an overriding unity, the concrete, immediate reality to a larger, less substantial abstraction. Genly begins to miss the shadows of Karhide. "There was something fluid, insubstantial in the very heaviness of this city built of monoliths, this monolithic state which called the part and the whole by the same name" (chap. 10).

As the Handdara stood behind the kingdom of Karhide, the Yomesh religion, with its stress on ultimate oneness, on the lack of division in time and space, stands behind the nation-state of Orgoreyn: "One center, one seeing, one law, one light." The Yomesh make the contrast of their world-view with that of Handdara explicit and unflattering: "In the sign of Meshe there is no darkness. Therefore those who call upon the darkness are made fools of and spat out from the mouth of Meshe, for they name what is not, calling it source and end" (chap. 12). As with all monisms, there is something emotionally and spiritually appealing; but monisms also, as William James points out, generally run counter to our experience of being in the world, and most often the ultimate principle of unity is kept vague and inaccessible.

The first two sections of the book, then, can be seen as antithetical on a variety of levels, revolving around the relationship between unity and diversity. As suggested already, though, these sections are not static tableaux: in the first we see a radical shift in the society itself; in the second, a significant change in Genly's perception of the situation. In the third section, process is even more crucial, for the focus is on the dynamics through which Genly and Therem form a relationship of optimum harmony through unity and separateness.

This section is set geographically and metaphorically both above and between Karhide and Orgoreyn, where the two humans are less bound by norms, attitudes, and restraints of any culture. This very separation leads to the fresh perceptions necessary for mutual understanding. Genly is able to see an exhausted, vulnerable Therem without the cultural envelopment of social role and custom:

> He wore nothing but his breeches; he was hot. The dark secret face was laid bare to the light, to my gaze. Estraven asleep looked a little stupid, like everyone else asleep: a round, strong face relaxed and remote, small drops of sweat on the upper lip and over the heavy eyebrows. I remembered how he had stood sweating on the parade-stand in Erhenrang in panoply of rank and sunlight. I saw him now defenseless and half naked in a colder light, and for the first time saw him as he was.
>
> (CHAP. 15)

An equivalent recognition on Therem's part is shown when he asks Genly about his family, and realizes that the Terran is as isolated in time as in space. Estraven says: "Long since in Erhenrang he had explained to me how time is shortened inside the ships that go almost as fast as starlight between the stars, but I had not laid this fact down against the length of a man's life or the lives he leaves behind him on his own world" (chap. 16). This realization is a particularly effective example of the first sentence of the book: one can "know" a fact but not fully apprehend it without the imagination.

The growing together continues, and can be said to reach a climax (or anticlimax) when Therem, sharing a small tent with Genly, enters kemmer. This crucial scene is one of the few places in the book where Genly has his own narrative overlap with Therem's, where the same incident is presented from both points of view. Some readers have seen the abstention from physical love-making as a failure of nerve or imagination on Le Guin's part. But in the context this article is trying to establish, Genly's explanation is an important key: "It was from the difference between us, not from the affinities and likenesses, but from the difference, that love came: and it was itself the bridge, the only bridge, across what divided us. For us to meet sexually would be for us to meet once more as aliens. We had touched, in the only way we could touch" (chap. 18). An accurate and sensitive realization of the differences as well as the similarities is central to the "I-Thou" relationship. The reason the hands match, both in "Tormer's Lay" and in the repeated motif of the tale "Estraven the Traitor," is not because they are identical but because they are different: left hand matches with right, right with left. This need for contrasts within harmony is underscored by Genly's use of the yin-yang symbol and by Estraven's comment: "It's queer that daylight's not enough. We need shadows, in order to walk" (chap. 19).

The important question, though, is whether the kind of relationship Genly and Therem form has any relevance in a large political and social context, whether the "I-Thou" bond has any meaning when there are many *I's* and *Thou's*. The structure of the book suggests a complex, tentative, partially tragic yes. For, although the protagonists cannot move their own relationship back into society — Therem, an exile, a person without a country, skis into the guns of Tibe's border patrol; and Genly reneges on a personal promise — these very acts of suicide and betrayal evince a tendency in the "I-Thou" relationship to move beyond its original two members, to encompass and expand rather than exclude. As Genly reasons: "I had said I would not bring the ship down till his banishment was ended, his name cleared. I could not throw away what he had died for, by insisting on the condition" (chap. 20).

More specifically, what Therem did die for was to bring the planet of Gethen into harmony — "Our border now is no line between two hills, but the line our planet makes in circling the Sun" (chap. 6) — and to have that planet take its place in an even larger unity, the Ekumen. Indeed, the Ekumen, whose goal is "the augmentation of the complexity and intensity of the field of intelligent life. The enrichment of harmony" (chap. 3), comes perhaps as close as any political system can to a viable reconciliation of unity and diversity, as suggested by the juxtaposition of the words "harmony" and "complexity." And it does this only by stressing what Genly learns in the course of the novel—the I-Thou relationship on the individual level must be ontologically prior and more valued than any unification on a larger scale. It is both beginning and basis. Towards the end of the book Genly says:

> Alone, I cannot change your world. But I can be changed by it. Alone, I must listen, as well as speak. Alone, the relationship I make, if I make one, is not impersonal and not only political: it is individual, it is personal. . . . So I was sent alone, for your sake? or for my own? I don't know.
>
> (CHAP. 8)

The question raised at the end of this passage echoes the opening of the novel when Genly wonders whose story it actually is. In the context of the entire book, the question is rhetorical: it is the story not primarily about single and separate entities but about the relations among them.

Weaving through the thesis-antithesis-synthesis structure sketched above is the alternation and interpenetration of fact and myth, the literal and the figurative. While this pattern is most obvious in the sections of myth, tales, and legends that seem to interrupt the central narrative, it is also discernible within that narrative itself. For example, the proverb used by Obsle—"We can pull a sledge together without being kemmerings" (chap. 6)—takes on a literal immediacy in the last part of the book. A movement in the opposite direction, from the literal to the figurative, can be seen in the use of the keystone. We first encounter it as a concrete fact in the opening scene, where King Argaven is mortaring a keystone between two piers, "making them one, one thing, an arch" (chap. 1). The repetition of "one" does create some resonance, but it is only later, at the beginning of the winter journey, that Genly explicitly associates certain qualities of mind with it, that object and action take on fuller symbolic reverberations. Looking at Estraven, Genly says: "He sat writing up his records with the same obdurate patient thoroughness I had seen in a mad king up on a scaffolding mortaring a joint, and said, '*When* we reach Karhide . . .'" (chap. 15). At the end of the book Genly uses the image without any reference to an actual scene—"I must set the keystone in the arch" (chap. 20) — yet it is only through the previous uses that the words rise above cliche and take on power. The approach here is what Charles Feidelson calls "symbolistic," where stress is put not only on the symbol as symbol, but on its origins, on its relations with the "real" world, on the very process of symbolization. The use of symbol, then, becomes a theme as well as a technique, where the epistemological complexities of how we experience the universe come to the fore.

The Left Hand of Darkness effectively uses science-fiction situations to explore some of these complexities. Other SF writers like Dick and Lem, and "mainstream" writers like Pynchon, Gaddis, Nabokov, and Borges, have created artistic visions that demonstrate our commonsense view of the world is merely an artificial construct, created primarily by language and other cultural preconceptions. Le Guin herself has spoken explicitly about this situation but, more importantly, embodies these insights in her fiction. For example, we hear Genly's conversation with the dying prisoner Asra at Pulefen Farm.

> Once I said, "I know about people who live on another world."
>
> "What kind of world would that be?"
>
> "One like this one, all in all; but it doesn't go around the sun. It goes around the star you call Selemy. That's a yellow star like the sun, and on that world, under that sun, live other people."
>
> "That's in the Sanovy teachings, that about the other worlds. There used to be an old Sanovy crazy-priest would come by my hearth when I was little and tell us children all about that, where the liars go when they die, and where the suicides go, and where the thieves go — that's where we're going, me and you, eh, one of those places?"
>
> "No, this I'm telling of isn't a spirit world. A real one. The people that live on it are real people, alive, just like here. But very-long-ago they learned how to fly."
>
> Asra grinned.
>
> (CHAP. 13)

Here we see that one man's legend may be another's homeland; one's life, another's story. That which seems occult, supernatural, fabulous may be due to lack of experience or knowledge, as is emphasized by Terra being the storied land, revolving about "a yellow star like the sun." On the positive side, the primary example of increasingly expanding

visions of the universe is the widening of range of each of the protagonists as their relationship develops. Genly realizes at one point:
"Until then I had rejected him [Therem], refused him his own reality"
(chap. 18).

Probably the most complex use of this sense of the multiplicity of
reality, of the reciprocal relation between "fact" and "myth," is the way
Gethenian legends, hearthtales, scriptures are used in the book. For example, Genly places prominently near the beginning the tale "The Place
Inside the Blizzard" not merely for the background it gives us about
Gethenian culture and values but because it is a condensed and displaced version of the main action: an exile encounters his dead sibling-
kemmering in a place away and apart from the society that makes them
outcasts. Later, Therem, in the literal counterpart of the "Place Inside
the Blizzard" encounters his dead sibling-kemmering Arek in the mindspeech of his new friend, Genly. Further, the names "Therem" and
"Arek" take on resonance from another hearthtale, located at the center
of the book, "Estraven the Traitor." Here we learn that "Therem" had
never been used as a name in Estre, until Arek of Estre and Therem of
Stok transgressed the feud between their domains and vowed kemmering. The ultimate result of this union is peace between the two lands, as
underscored by the Therem of the longer narrative mentioning a
journey he once took with "four of our friends, from Stok" (chap. 15).

This kind of interaction among myth and legend and narrative
comes full circle when Genly, at the end of the novel, brings Therem's
journals to his native hearth, there to be incorporated in the domain's
records, later, perhaps, to become the stuff of future legends and tales.
Indeed, in the last paragraph, Therem's father asks us to hear the "tale"
of how Genly and his son crossed the Gobrin ice, while Therem's son
eagerly asks Genly for the kind of story about "other worlds out among
the stars" (chap. 20) that had puzzled and bored the dying Asra. While
formerly the myths could be seen as interpolations within a more
"realistic" narrative, we begin to wonder if Genly's suggestion in the first
sentence, of making his report as if he told a story, contains a truth we
may have missed at first, a truth suggested by Borges' parable about the
Quixote.

> The whole scheme of the work consisted in the opposition of
> the two worlds: the unreal world of books of chivalry, the or-
> dinary everyday world of the seventeenth century.
> They did not suspect that the years would finally smooth

away that discord, they did not suspect that La Mancha and Montiel and the knight's lean figure would be, for posterity, no less poetic than the episodes of Sinbad or the vast geographies of Ariosto.

For in the beginning of literature is the myth, and in the end as well.

Myth, Exchange and History in *The Left Hand of Darkness*

Jeanne Murray Walker

The theories of Claude Lévi-Strauss provide an access to understanding the workings of the myths in Ursula Le Guin's *The Left Hand of Darkness* (*LHD*). Among other things, the French anthropologist calls attention to the oppositional structure of myth and to its function in social exchange. He points out that myths are a particularly valuable key to the collective thought of a society because they offer an unusually clear code which classifies and interrelates the data of social experience of the peoples to whom those myths belong. They reinforce and verify the economic, cosmological, and kinship norms of a given society in compressed, almost algebraic fashion. The myths reflect, and reflect upon, the problems and contradictions which arise in practical, everyday life. According to Lévi-Strauss, such thought, inevitably, is highly structured. Myth incorporates in story form pairs of images which represent contradictions lying at the center of the society. The story then develops in such a way as to allow those oppositions common ground. It qualifies or mediates their differences. By mediating between opposites, as they cannot be mediated in real life, myth temporarily overcomes contradiction.

The relationship Lévi-Strauss outlines between myth and lived experience (or human-history) corresponds to that between the chapters in *LHD* which are distinctly mythic and others which might be called historical. The myths in *LHD*, it can be assumed, represent the collective thought of Karhidian and Orgotan societies, respectively, about their most vital and puzzling social dilemmas. They are, in fact, models

From *Science-Fiction Studies* 6, no. 2 (July 1979).©1979 by SFS Publications.

which share many of the symbols, themes, and names found elsewhere in the fiction. That these myths have many narrators (e.g., "Estraven the Traitor") or that their narrators remain unknown (e.g., "The Place Inside the Blizzard") indicates that they have been distilled and shaped by an entire society. Bearing the authority of the social collective (commanding, that is, the broad assent of the contemporaries and also of ancestors) these myths assume a normative function in the novel. By means of them the most crucial social problems touched upon in *LHD* can be identified and the ideal solutions to those problems defined. Furthermore, the underlying structure of the myths — the reconciliation of opposites — typifies the structure of *LHD* as a whole. Thus the myths both anticipate and act as ideal models for the "historical" events in Le Guin's fiction.

If the *process* Lévi-Strauss pinpoints in myth is mediation of opposites, the *theme* he finds at the heart of myth is the social version of that process: exchange. Exchange between human beings in effect constitutes society. Such exchange takes place at the economic level, when people swap goods and services; at the linguistic level, when they give words to one another in conversation; or at the level of kinship, when they marry into one another's families. Each kind of exchange is governed by rules which vary from one society to another. The value of exchange goes far beyond that of the items involved: the exchanges an individual makes, when taken together, form a pattern which defines his social status, his role. Therefore, each individual is the sum and product of the social exchanges in which he participates, and no individual can avoid being defined in this way since no individual can totally escape social exchange.

Of all exchanges, those which define kinship are the most basic. As Lévi-Strauss points out, "the rules of kinship and marriage are not made necessary by the social state. They *are* the social state itself, reshaping biological relationships and natural sentiments, forcing them into structures implying them as well as others, and compelling them to rise above their original characteristics." Societies depend for their very existence on kinship rules — rules of descent, rules about dwelling, prohibition of incest, and so on. Even more importantly, kinship rules, which almost universally prohibit incest, force the biological family to extend itself, to ally itself with other families. Because of the incest prohibition (a negative rule) and the prescription for legitimate partners (a positive rule) marriage results in complex alliances arising among human beings. Such alliances are essential if families are to endure, for food and shelter and physical defense require larger units than single families. Kinship alliances insure that the interests of individuals will lie in supporting the group and ultimately in sustaining the society.

Unlike the openended corpus of actual myths that anthropologists examine, the corpus of myths in *LHD* is closed and complete. Therefore, it is possible to analyze the entire set of Gethenian myths and establish the ways in which they are connected. Kinship exchange, in the Lévi-Strauss sense, comprises their dominant theme. In them, Le Guin articulates the theme of exchange by employing contrary images — heat and cold, dark and light, home and exile, name and namelessness, life and death, murder and sex — so as finally to reconcile their contrariety. The myths present wholeness, or unity, as an ideal; but that wholeness is never merely the integrity of an individual who stands apart from society. Instead, it consists of the tenuous and temporary integration of individuals into social units.

The Orgota creation myth investigates beginnings, locating the origin of man between pairs of unstable oppositions. "In the beginning there was nothing but ice and sun" (chap. 18). Under duress of the sun, the ice gave way, melting into three great iceshapes. The iceshapes created the world and ultimately sacrificed themselves ("let the sun melt them") to give men consciousness. With consciousness, however; came fear. Edondurath, the tallest and the eldest of the men, awoke first and fearing the others, killed thirty-eight of his thirty-nine brothers. With their bodies he built a hut in which he waited for the thirty-ninth, who had escaped him. That last and youngest brother returned when Edondurath lay in Kemmer and they coupled, engendering the nations of men. Edondurath asked his kemmering why each of the men was followed by a piece of darkness, to which his kemmering replied:

> Because they were born in the house of flesh, therefore death follows at their heels. They are in the middle of time. In the beginning there was the sun and the ice, and there was no shadow. In the end when we are done, the sun will devour itself, and shadow will eat light, and there will be nothing left but the ice and darkness.
>
> (CHAP. 17)

This myth explicates that essential mystery, creation, in a way which emphasizes the difference between men as social creatures and men as isolated individuals. Edondurath, the oldest, "the first to wake up," behaves in a totally isolating egocentric way. Because he fears his brothers when he sees them begin to waken, he kills them, thereby eliminating the necessity of confronting them as individualities. Then, to build himself a dwelling, he stacks them up like objects, which they are because he has refused to accord them the status of conscious beings. Into this dwelling comes a being who is his opposite both because he is youngest and because he is sexually different. The biological urgency of Edondurath's kemmer results in his integration with this other human consciousness. The language of the myth suggests that such biological intercourse brings about social intercourse. "Of these two were the *nations of men* born" (chap. 17; emphasis added). When men exist in nations—that is, in society—they exist in time, or more precisely "in the middle of time." So the creation myth equates the temporal median with social mediation. Social exchange is the invariable condition of men in time; the lack of exchange—totally egocentric behavior—is equated with nonbeing at the beginning and end of time.

The logic of man's social exchange is further explicated in "The Place Inside the Blizzard." Two brothers in the androgynous world of Gethen vow kemmering for life, a vow which is illegal. In the Hearth of Shath, where they live, brothers may stay together only until they have produced one child. The brothers produce a child. Then the Lord of Shath commands them to break their vow. One brother despairs and commits suicide. The other, Getheren, assigned the great public shame of the suicide, suffers exile. He departs Shath to seek his death on the ice, but before he goes he thrusts his name and his guilt onto the town. Then, wandering deep on the Pering ice, Getheren meets his brother, all white and cold, who asks him to remain and keep their vow. Getheren declines, replying that when his brother chose death, he broke the vow. The brother tries to clutch Getheren, seizing him by the left hand. Getheren flees and several days later he is discovered in a province which neighbors Shath, speechless. He recovers, but his frozen arm must be amputated. Then he leaves for southern lands, calling himself Ennoch. During his long stay there, no crops will grow in Shath. When Ennoch finally becomes an old man, he tells his story to a kinsman from Shath and reclaims the name Getheren. Immediately, thereafter he dies, whereupon Shath returns to prosperity.

The brothers' crime is loving one another so excessively that they exclude the community. Because they swear permanent vows to one another, their love is defined by law as a crime. Lifelong incest is prohibited, but not for the biologically based reason that incest results in weakened offspring (on Gethen brothers are permitted to produce offspring). Rather, lifelong vows of sexual loyalty between brothers are prohibited because they prevent vows with others outside the family. In *The Elementary Structures of Kinship* Lévi-Strauss makes this point:

> Exchange — and consequently the rule of exogamy which expresses it — has in itself a social value. It provides the means of binding men together, and of superimposing upon the natural links of kinship the henceforth artificial links — artificial in the sense that they are removed from chance encounters or the promiscuity of family life — of alliance governed by rule.

Exchange of permanent marriage vows is the most significant of all social exchanges, since it knits the participants together in mutual obligation and in concern for their offspring. The vows which bind men of different families create a complex network of loyalties and interrelationships which define the Hearth. Without such a network, based on exchange, the Hearth could not function cohesively; it would disintegrate into solitary, isolated — perhaps warring — families. Therefore, the law which requires sexual exchange is fundamental to the existence of the Hearth.

This law of the community competes with the powerful human desire for personal integrity: the need "to keep to oneself." Keeping to oneself is Lévi-Strauss's pun: it means both remaining isolated, alone, and retaining one's kin by not allowing them to marry outside the family. The brothers' need to keep to each other in the intimacy of the sexual act is so strong that they vow kemmering to one another for life, thereby defying the law which is fundamental to the continued existence of the Hearth. They force a deadlock between the existence of self and the existence of the social group. When the Lord of the Hearth breaks the deadlock in favor of the social group, one of the brothers performs the ultimate act of keeping to himself: he commits suicide, thereby depriving the social group of all further exchange with him. Thus suicide repudiates the law of exchange which makes social groups in *LHD* possible.

Once the individual places himself at odds with the community, the balance shifts back and forth between the individual and the community until one or the other is destroyed. The community defines the absolute repudiation of exchange — the suicide of the brother — as the worst possible crime and lays the guilt for this crime on Getheren, the remaining brother. On Getheren the Hearth levies exile, the punishment which fits the crime. Exile robs Getheren of the right to exchange anything with his community, as his brother's suicide had robbed the community of the right to exchange anything with him. In response, Getheren bestows his name on the Hearth.

In this myth, as is the case more explicitly in Le Guin's *Earthsea* trilogy, an individual's name signifies his identity, his moral credits and debits. Therefore, when Getheren curses the Hearth with his name, he, on the one hand, transfers responsibility for the suicide of the brother to the Hearth and on the other denies himself identity as an individual. His journey to the Ice signals his movement away from the community to himself. The center of the ice, the place inside the blizzard, signifies absolute lack of community, a place where "we who kill ourselves dwell" (chap. 2), as the brother says. Such absolute isolation is rejected by Getheren. He takes an alternative name and identity, participating in another society as "Ennoch." Meanwhile, the Hearth, which enforced its own rule of exchange at great cost to one of its members, undergoes famine. This lack of physical sustenance is a metaphor for the lack of social sustenance which occurs when a member of a social group cannot participate in its activities of exchange. The group experiences deprivation and potentially death. But when Getheren hears of the famine in the Hearth he reassumes his name and with it, responsibility for the suicide of his brother. His own death, restoring plenty to the Hearth, follows immediately.

The mutual dependence between a group and its members is so imperative, the myth shows, that death follows when that dependence is denied. Human beings have urgent needs both for privacy and for communal exchanges. As the contradiction between the brother's vows and the law of Hearth demonstrates, these needs are sometimes mutually exclusive. When they are, the rule of exchange must override the need to keep to oneself. If the rule of exchange is broken, someone must pay. The community in the myth tries to make Getheren pay by exiling him, while Getheren tries to make the community pay by cursing it with his name. The community cannot survive in health with its law of exchange thus challenged. Getheren himself can survive only by assuming a role and joining another community — that is, by reaffirming the social law of exchange. In the end, Getheren, rather than the Hearth, assumes responsibility for the suicide which denied the law of exchange. When he bears the guilt he removes its onus from the Hearth. But the myth clearly shows that if he had not done so the whole community might have perished. The vow of the brothers initiates a *negative* exchange — the suicide, the exile, and the curse. The myth shows that such denials of the law of exchange result in the death of either the individual or the community because both individuals and communities require exchange, not merely for psychological health, but for continued existence.

A third myth in *LHD* explores the logic of exchange in a broader context, between rather than within communities. Involved here is a dispute over land between the Domain of Stok and the Domain of Estre (chap. 9). One day Arek, the heir of Estre, skating over the ice, falls in, barely pulls himself out, stumbles to a cabin nearby, and is discovered nearly dead from the cold by Therem, the heir of Stok. Therem brings Arek back to life by warming him with his own body. When the two lay their hands together, they match. The two mortal enemies swear kemmering together. After several days some of Therem's countrymen of Stok come to the hut and, seeing Arek, murder him. But after a year, someone arrives at the door of Arek's father, hands him a child, and tells him "This is Therem, the son's son of Estre." Many years later this young man, who has been named heir of Estre, is attacked on the ice by his three brothers, who wish to reign themselves. All but dead from his fight with them he enters a hut. There Therem of Stok binds the wounds of Therem of Estre. Their hands match and they vow peace. When Therem of Estre recovers and, after many years, becomes ruler of Estre, he gives half the disputed lands to Stok and reconciles the two domains. Because of this action he is called Estraven the Traitor.

Here the concept of exchange is demonstrated positively rather than negatively; the ideal of unity is achieved, but at a price. The young heirs, because they belong to warring domains, are not merely strangers but mortal enemies. Yet instead of perpetuating destructive exchange between their domains, they vow kemmering. Because they are the heirs of their repective domains, their doing so mediates, metonymically, the quarrel over the lands. Yet each respective domain refuses to follow the rule of the heirs, preferring instead the rule of the domain, which, in order to protect its own people and customs, denies the value of any others. To this rule of exclusivity the heirs' love is sacrificed: Arek is murdered and that act permanently separates the two heirs. Yet, because Therem of Stok gives the son of that union to Estre, the breach between the domains is healed. The warring communities are reconciled by that gift, the son of the two enemies' love. His very name, Therem of Estre, mediates between the two domains. His ironic title, "Estraven the Traitor," signifies the sacrifice involved in any system of positive exchange between communites, between competing social systems. In order for a man to reconcile competing social systems it is necessary to transcend the definition of both — that is, he must sacrifice his own social definition and status in either.

A fourth myth, "On Time and Darkness," describes Orgota's god, Meshe, who is said to be the center of time, the universal One. This ideal of the One, which is apparent in the symbol of Meshe, stands behind all the myths in *LHD,* and also behind the historical sections of the novel. In the historical sections the ideal appears as both the political ideal, the Ekumen, and the personal ideal, human intimacy. These ideals are social, not supernatural. Rafail Nudelman has argued that the figure of Meshe, like other symbols in *LHD,* implies a "second universe" where "objects and phenomena lay bare their hidden universal significance and supra-historical law of being." But Le Guin's myth relates to human beings. "We are the pupils of his Eye. Our doing is his Seeing: our being is his Knowing" (chap. 12). Meshe is suprahistorical only in the sense that he is an imagined, mythical character. He is the image of exchange, which brings about the unification of individuals into communities and of communities into states and of states into the Ekumen. This kind of exchange may represent an ideal whose attainment is difficult, perhaps impossible; but is is not supernatural.

LHD finally rejects all static versions of the ideal, all temptations to escape time, even in its myths. The latter do not follow the tautological pattern either of the eternal return or of the eternal wandering. Instead, they define alienation within and between communities and then, without engaging in perfectly ideal solutions, demonstrate healthy systems of social exchange at work. The exchange is presumably endless, for new selves emerge, new choices are made, new oppositions are defined in the continuing process of history. And so new unities must be constantly achieved. These unities are fragile and momentary. Perfect coalition between men in *LHD* cannot be formalized in documents or solidified in government structures. Yet, as "On Time and Darkness" shows, such perfect coalition exists as a permanent ideal.

The myths of Getheren serve as a means for exploring the ideal of exchange by first embodying contradictories and then reconciling them. But the same myths also reflect normative patterns of exchange which actually appear in the "historical" sections of *LHD.* Estraven's unwillingness to pursue Karhide's interest in the Shinoath border dispute repeats the action of his ancestor, "Estraven the Traitor," who gave half the disputed land to Stok. "Estraven the Traitor" also predicts and illustrates the sacrifice involved in initiating such an exchange. Estraven fails as his ancestor, Therem of Stok, failed; before Karhide and Orgota unite,

Estraven actually dies in the cause, as his ancestor, Arek of Estre, died. Before dying, he suffers the indignity of exile, recapitulating the pattern of "The Place Inside the Blizzard." Although the actions recounted in that myth replicate those of the novel's historical section, their meaning is there reversed. Estraven is exiled from Karhide not for "keeping to himself," an act which actually challenges the social system, but rather for exactly the opposite, for political exchange with a stranger. His exile leads to his journey on the ice. There, in a place inside the blizzard he meets Genly Ai: not a brother, but a stranger. In this intimate place they discover how to "mindspeak" one another's names. The exile Estraven, who bears responsibility for initiating not only his own but his country's exchange with the stranger, dies like the exile Getheren, who bears responsibility for refusing to exchange. Ironically, the penalty of initiating exchange and for refusing to exchange is the same. This is because too much exchange with "strangers"—those outside the community—produces the same outcome as too little exchange within the community. In either case, the community feels cheated of the full benefit of its member. Thus the pattern of exchange which the myths set up is repeated—sometimes with ironic outcome, sometimes not—in the historical content of the novel.

Other patterns set up in the mythic sections of *LHD* are also repeated in the historical ones. Although the history is told by specific perceivers, it is told by two distinct voices: an "alien" and a "traitor." Early in the book Genly Ai instructs the reader that the many voices are "all one, and if at moments the facts seem to alter with an altered voice, why then you can choose the fact you like best: yet none of them are false, and it is all one story" (chap. 1). This corresponds to the collective voice which the myths in the novel assume. Furthermore, the symbols in the historical sections are conspicuously the same as those in the myths: in both, Le Guin employs the same (aforementioned) contraries.

Most importantly the patterns set up in the myths serve as rules which guide and define the behavior of characters in the historical section. For example, when Estraven learns of his exile from Karhide, he considers returning home to Estre, but he does not. Instead, he quickly concludes "I was born to live in exile and my one way home [is] by way of dying." This easy conclusion seems not to tally with his courageous, stubborn political behavior in Karhide. But shortly after this episode we discover that his self-exile may have more to do with real guilt over incestuous vows than with the trumped-up political charge that he is a traitor. Estraven remarks to his kemmering that their vows were false because "the only true vow of faithfulness I ever swore was not spoken, nor could it be spoken" (chap. 6). Much later, at the conclusion of the novel, we discover that Estraven's earlier "true vow of faithfulness" was made to his brother. The vow, even though it is never verbalized, represents Estraven's reluctance to participate in the most important aspect of social exchange, the importance of which the reader will know from having read "The Place Inside the Blizzard." Accepting the logic of that myth, Estraven judges himself guilty and himself enforces the penalty which the myth prescribes, exile and eventual death. Of course, Estraven's guilt involves an intention, not an act. But the important thing is that the myths provide both the characteristics in the historical sections and the reader with rules for judging human behavior and with the logic behind such rules.

The most important rule is that of exchange, and its paradigmatic figure in the historical section of the novel is Faxe the Weaver. He shows that is is possible to connect categorically unique human beings in religious ritual. Early in the novel Genly Ai describes this ritual, which thrives on "an old darkness, passive, anarchic, silent" (chap. 5). Genly Ai himself becomes drawn into the web, which is masterfully woven and controlled by Faxe. This weaving ritual of brilliant intuitive intensity is paralleled very late in the book by Faxe's cool appearance as a politician in Karhide, expediting the official exchanges between citizens. Faxe the Weaver is the Karhidian equivalent of the Orgoreyn god, Meshe. At the level of politics and at the level of religion he promotes exchange—in some sense he symbolizes exchange. But is is always in history, in real human events not in some distant unchanging place or time.

The novel's imagery of the weaver and weaving shows that any ideal which attempts to fix the movement of time or to make human relationships rigid must be suspect. Productive human exchanges which weave people together into healthy communities are contrasted in the novel with quick, superficial unity: Estraven is replaced in Karhide by Tibe, whose dramatic appeals for unity depend upon his cooked-up threat of war. His superficial resemblance to both Meshe and Faxe the Weaver shows in his face, which is "masked with a net of fine wrinkles" (chap. 8). However, Tibe's face, along with his communications network, the radio, parodies the book's true relationships. A second parody of the novel's ideal becomes evident in the houses of Mishnory, which are "all built to a pattern" (chap. 8). The mesh is distorted into an optical illusion, focusing not on the connecting strands, but on the boxes they form. It emphasizes the emptiness, the vacuity, the unproductiveness of rigid order. Such rigidity is manifest in the Orgotan way of categorizing people and keeping track of them with papers. But perhaps the most powerful representation of unproductive human relationships is the cold trip Genly Ai takes with twenty-six silent Orgotians in the back of a truck which he describes as a "steel box" (chap. 13). In it he is taken to Pulefen Farm, where he and the other prisoners are kept in dull conformity by anti-kemmer drugs. Such imagery represents social ideals which do not take account of real exchange. Without such exchange the social structure calcifies and becomes rigid. According to Estraven, who brings about personal and political unity, that unity must be brought out of change: "The unexpected is what makes life possible," he tells Genly Ai (chap. 8). And he confesses in his notebook that his one gift is the ability to take advantage of flux and change: "I never had a gift but one, to know when the great wheel gives to a touch, to know and act" (chap. 14). Illegitimate unity suffocates, the novel shows; legitimate unity arises out of spontaneous human exchange.

Most crucially, then, the myths in *LHD* assert the impossibility of retreating from history and from human society. They insist that the goal of "keeping to oneself" in a fixed, temporal place is an impossible fantasy, a fantasy that must be sacrificed to the demands of communal exchange in history. This is implied by the pattern of exchange, the mediating of opposites, which underlies all myths. Truth arises out of conflict; the only legitimate unity is fragile and momentary. So Le Guin rejects static, cyclical structures. In her myths, as in myths which Lévi-Strauss interprets, the oppositions define human problems, particularly problems with exchange; their mediation creates or maintains community. That these myths are fundamental to the meaning of the book is evident in the fact that the patterns they define account for most of the plot in the historical sections of the novel. The novel thus locates significance not in some static, timeless place, but in history; and its myths reflect social ideals which continually — and with difficulty — emerge from that history.

Determinism, Free Will, and Point of View in Le Guin's *The Left Hand of Darkness*

The heart of Ursula K. Le Guin's novel, *The Left Hand of Darkness,* at least from a Western point of view, is a paradox. To borrow the title metaphor, on one hand the book seems to teach us how fully determined is the world in which we imagine ourselves, our attitudes and destinies controlled by accidents of sex, of environment, and even of language. On the other hand, the book is clearly didactic, urging us implicitly to will away the imperatives of biology, of physics, and even of our minds. Determinism and free will are classic antagonists in our philosophic tradition, and one cannot, of course, have things both ways. In every respect the left and the right reverse each other. The Western, scientific, Aristotelian point of view is that one can trace the sequences of cause and effect and come to understand the roots of how things are by learning how they were determined. To work within the deterministic assumptions of Western culture would seem to destroy the possibility of free will. But in Le Guin's artistic practice, and in the philosophy of the Eastern world, the left hand and the right form a unity by virtue of their difference. Whether one sees reversal as antagonism or fulfillment is, in a profound sense, a matter of point of view. By manipulating the reader's expected acceptance of the importance of determinism, Le Guin channels his mind into a new direction. This direction is not the simple reversal of determinism, the celebration of free will, but a coordination — to use the Ekumen's term — of determinism and free will within a wider concept, point of view itself. Le Guin's remarkable

From *Extrapolation* 20, no. 1 (Spring 1979).©1979 by the Kent State University Press.

achievement is that she can manipulate our habitual point of view so that we come to see things from a new point of view, that for which point of view itself is central.

The most famous — and obvious — determinism explored in this novel is sexual. Each Gethenian is sexually inactive during most of each month ("somer"), but when the period of estrus comes ("kemmer"), a person becomes a highly active male or female, the physiological development depending on the state of those around "him."

> The kemmer phenomenon fascinates all of us Investigators, of course. It fascinates us, but it rules the Gethenians, dominates them. The structure of their societies, the management of their industry, agriculture, commerce, the size of their settlements, the subjects of their stories, everything is shaped to fit the somer-kemmer cycle. . . .
>
> Consider: Anyone can turn his hand to anything. This sounds very simple, but its psychological effects are incalculable. The fact that everyone between seventeen and thirty-five or so is liable to be . . . "tied down to childbearing," implies that no one is quite so thoroughly "tied down" here as women, elsewhere, are likely to be — psychologically or physically. Burden and privilege are shared out pretty equally; everybody has the same risk to run or choice to make. Therefore nobody here is quite so free as a free male anywhere else.

In keeping with the determinism inherent in her exposition of this situation, Le Guin indeed shapes the society, industry and even folk tales of Gethen to reflect this biological fact. Such tailoring is not of value merely for itself, however, but to further certain philosophic ends. "'Fundamentally Terra and Gethen are very much alike'" and so we are to draw conclusions about our own world from our insight into this other world. As Le Guin writes in her introduction, "Science fiction is not predictive; it is descriptive." The world she describes, despite its admitted oddities, is, beneath the appearances, our own.

In order to help us beneath those appearances, she provides us with one normally sexed human being, Genly Ai, a black man from Terra who is the "Mobile" of the Ekumen sent to invite Gethen to join the confraternity of inhabited worlds. As the Investigators had noted in scouting the planet,

The First Mobile, if one is sent, must be warned that unless he is very self-assured, or senile, his pride will suffer. A man wants his virility regarded, a woman wants her femininity appreciated, however indirect and subtle the indications of regard and appreciation. On Winter [English for Gethen] they will not exist. One is respected and judged only as a human being. It is an appalling experience.

And Genly Ai is duly appalled — and confused and mistaken. Yet, at the same time that Le Guin is exposing a deterministic situation, it is clear from her very exposition that she invites the exercise of free will to overcome it. Surely it is more important to be judged "as a human being" than as either a man or as a woman; surely we would not want to misread people as Genly Ai does simply because we are overly fixated on mere matters of sex. Yet, it must be admitted that sex does determine a great deal about a person and "'It's extremely hard to separate the innate differences from the learned ones.'" How then to see beneath appearances? Typically in this novel, it is by rising above them, seeking a wider context:

In the end, the dominant factor in Gethenian life is not sex or any other human thing: it is their environment, their cold world. Here man has a crueler enemy even than himself.

In switching our attention from the determinism of sex to the determinism of environment, Le Guin is forcing us to change our point of view.

Genly Ai postulates that the killing cold of Gethen makes survival so chancy that the institution of war is counteradaptive. Thus, the Gethenians' lack of such an institution might be "explained" by environmental determinism. Certainly Genly Ai, whose point of view we ought most to share, explains Gethenian law in that way: "Life on Winter is hard to live, and people there generally leave death to nature or to anger, not to law." He even explains the failures of imagination by reference to the environment: why don't Gethenians have flying machines? "How would it ever occur to a sane man that he could fly?" Estraven said sternly. It was a fair response, on a world where no living thing is winged." Even Estraven, the Gethenian, indulges in deterministic explanation. In predicting the weather for the impending cross-glacial trek, Estraven explains that

"The good weather, you know, tends to stay over the great glaciers, where the ice reflects the heat of the sun; the storms are pushed out to the periphery. Therefore the legends about the Place inside the Blizzard."

The key word here is "therefore": determinism seems to explain everything, whether it be a determinism of sex or a determinism of environment.

Le Guin goes much further than these explicit passages in validating determinism. If she is overtly creating a world in which the existence of a certain folk narrative is explained, then she can actualize that world by offering the folk narrative itself as part of the novel. She does this in chapter 2. What must be remembered, however, is that nothing *determines* that Le Guin will offer such a tale: she makes it up out of her own mind and we readers who recognize that we are involved with fiction know it to be made up. As readers we admire the skill that not only presents the story in the "folk" form but later justifies it meterologically. We also respond, even if only unconsciously, to the obviously conscious patterning of the novel that comes about in part through the reuse of this image: in the folk narrative of "Estraven the Traitor," the hut in which Arek and Therem meet is a place inside the blizzard, in the Orgota creation myth, the house of corpses is a place inside the blizzard, and in the story of the glacier-crossing, the tent in which Therem and Genly Ai first mindspeak is a place inside the blizzard. In the original folk narrative, the place appears at first as both good and bad since it is both the locale of a desired reunion and the land of death. What shall be our point of view on it? As Terrans — Westerners — we are confused, but upon re-reading, after having come to understand that suicide is a paramount crime on Gethen, we realize that such a death is irredeemable in all cases. Hence the boon of reunion tips the balance toward good. On a first reading we would not see this, not yet having learned to adopt a Gethenian point of view, but we learn to adopt such a point of view by reading the novel. In understanding the tale of "Estraven the Traitor," the hut must be seen by Westerners as good because it supports a strong conventional value: the conquest of family feuds by love. If we have been raised on *Romeo and Juliet*, we know what point of view to take on this place in the blizzard. Then in the Orgota creation myth, the hut of corpses, manifestly a place of death, is made the place of creation. Thus, the connectedness of life and death is added to our previous approbation of the image of the place inside the blizzard. To this point of view we may add, among other values, the traditional value of honesty in the mindspeaking episode because mindspeech allows for no lies. Hence, when all this is followed by a meteorological explanation, what is a matter of chosen — manipulated — point of view has come also to seem a determined part of the narrative world. Hence, our recollection of the folk narrative confirms both determinism and free will: the tale as such is fit but its inclusion and narrative uses are matters of choice. By implication, Le Guin shows us that both fitness and choice depend on point of view.

She is similarly subtle in her incidental creation of cultural artifacts:

> On a world where a common table implement is a little device
> with which you crack the ice that has formed on your drink
> between drafts, hot beer is a thing you come to appreciate.

Of course, there is no such world; there are no such artifacts. Le Guin makes up the world and then, instead of saying "it was so cold that they had to serve table implements to crack the ice off their drinks," she turns matters around, assumes in a deterministic way what the implements would be in such a world, and then has Genly Ai observe not the fitness of the implement but the fitness of the warm drink. Thus, the fitness of the implement is tacit and serves to increase our sense of a deterministic world without the need of explicit speculations such as those of the Investigators.

Perhaps the subtlest tactics of all are exhibited in the very language of the novel, as indeed they should be since novels, finally, are made of nothing but words. We are told, in the overt way we have already noted, that

> Gethenians often think in thirteens, twenty-sixes, fifty-twos,
> no doubt because of the 26-day lunar cycle that makes their
> unvarying month and approximates their sexual cycles.

This explicit observation is implicit later in Estraven's narration: "Forgery of papers is risky in Orgoreyn where they are inspected fifty-two times daily." An American would say, for whatever cultural reasons, "one hundred" or "a thousand" while a Frenchman would say "thirty-six," but the canonical number for exaggeration in Karhidish is obviously fifty-two. That this is fit is determined by the earlier, overt observation about thinking in thirteens; that Le Guin chose to actualize that observation in this way is a matter of personal, and highly skillful, choice.

Other factors of environment also determine the language of this novel. The enormous importance of keen meteorological observation for survival on Gethen is reflected in both Karhidish and Orgota having numerous words for many different types and conditions of snow, sleet, and so on. The parallel fact about Eskimo is often adduced by linguists to indicate that Eskimos actually see more distinctions among snowfalls than, say, speakers of English. The suggestion in that language is not only shaped by reality but conversely shapes it is known as the Sapir-Whorf hypothesis:

> The relation between language and experience is often misunderstood. Language is not merely a more or less systematic inventory of the various items of experience which seem relevant to the individual, as is so often naïvely assumed, but is also a self-contained, creative symbolic organization, which not only refers to experience largely acquired without its help but actually defines experience for us by reason of its formal completeness and because of our unconscious projection of its implicit expectations into the field of experience.

Genly Ai implicitly accepts this hypothesis as true when he wonders "How could I explain the Age of the Enemy, and its aftereffects, to a people who had no word for war?" Le Guin implicitly accepts this hypothesis by creating and using such terms as "kemmer" and "shifgrethor" and "hieb" and "nusuth" and "dothe," by constructing an elaborate "Gethenian Calendar and Clock," and then by using its terminology throughout the novel. Thus is a Gethenian reality created, freely chosen and thereafter determined. In an implicit and thus profound way, reading the language of this novel makes one adopt a point of view that accepts the notion that one can at least in part choose how one's world is determined.

The delineation of point of view is often a problem in understanding language and is a central problem in this novel. Let us consider, for example, the word "traitor." Like the image of the place inside the blizzard, "traitor" is part of the pattern of the novel. Thus, it both determines and is determined while its several artistic uses imply the will behind the work. This word first occurs when Argaven addresses the Stabiles on Hain via ansible, a communications machine, "'Ask your machine there what makes a man a traitor.'" The answer comes, finally: "'I do not know what makes a man a traitor. No man considers himself a traitor: this makes it hard to find out.'" Although some readers may believe that some traitors know themselves as such, the text clearly asks us to accept this as a wise answer. If we do, we see that it puts point of view even above the question of language. When Ashe approaches Genly Ai after Estraven's exile in hopes of getting the Mobile to being money to the deposed Prime Minister, Genly Ai does not know who is meant when Ashe calls himself "'a friend of one who befriended you'" because he has never understood that Estraven was his friend. Hence we readers, knowing Genly Ai's ignorance and Ashe's devotion, read the irony in Ashe's clarification: "'Estraven, the traitor.'" From the point of view of the character, which we must momentarily adopt, the word is a stigma wrongly applied by the king. In the folk narrative called "Estraven the Traitor," the title character is a traitor because he ceded land to the neighboring Domain of Stok and thus ended a feud. However, from our point of view he is no traitor, first because his birth was the result of placing humanity over politics when his mother-to-be gave help to his sorely disabled father-to-be and second because the cession of territory is precisely what Estraven with whom we are concerned, and whom we admire, suggests as a solution to the conflict over the Sinoth Valley. In both cases, moreover, from a wider point of view than that of the Domain or of Karhide, from the point of view of the Ekumen, the acts of cession would restore order and serve a wider human purpose than aggrandizement: peace. Understanding this point of view, we see that Estraven has fully understood the Ekumenical point of view when he can be self-ironic in making plans with Genly Ai to bring down the Star Ship and promise to keep himself out of sight for a while since "'I am Estraven the Traitor. I have nothing to do with you." Since Genly Ai and Estraven have come to share a point of view, they have a common use of the language and thus can say without misunderstanding that Thessicher, who turns Estraven into Tibe, is a "traitor." And finally, we understand the bitterness of loss which Genly Ai nearly indulges by putting himself before his dead friend after Estraven's self-sacrifice: "the traitor. He had gone on by himself, deserting me, deserting me." Depending on point of view, a word can mean so many things.

Le Guin uses the language of the novel to determine her readers' points of view, manipulating us and leading us from beginning to end. For example, we come to accept the possibility of paradoxical truth through the many aphorisms in the novel. "'The admirable is inexplicable.'" The aphorisms themselves often implicitly support the determinism we have seen in the vocabulary and usage practices of the novel.

"'The Glaciers didn't freeze overnight.'" "'We must sully the plain snow with footprints, in order to get anywhere.'" These are the sayings of a frigid world. Le Guin deterministically justifies a narrative world fraught with aphorism:

> Estraven [told] the whole tale of our crossing of the Ice . . . as only a person of an oral-literature tradition can tell a story, so that it becomes a saga, full of traditional locutions.

Yet, here again we see determinism implicitly serving the will of the author, for Le Guin's novel itself is told with traditional locutions, the aphorisms we are reading, and yet comes from a purely fictive realm. This is a paradox which we feel quite as strongly as we might feel the paradoxical truth of any of the aphorisms themselves.

Just as the environment may determine the language, the characters may determine language. And just as Le Guin turns the former process around by first assuming the world with the ice-cracking table implement, so she turns character around by first conceiving the characters and then having them speak as their characteristics ought to determine. Yet, of course, their speeches are chosen by Le Guin — and we know it. Estraven, who is clearly the noblest character in the book and most in touch with his world, speaks in aphorisms of his own invention: "'Do you know the saying, *Karhide is not a nation but a family quarrel?* I haven't [sic], and I suspect that Estraven made it up; it has his stamp.'" Estraven is similarly pithy in distilling the experience of his exile: "'Banished men should never speak their native tongue; it comes bitter from their mouth.'" By contrast, Tibe and Obsle, both of whom oppose Estraven at the book's political level, must self-consciously borrow their aphorisms: "poor relations must be in good time, as the saying is, eh?" and "we can pull a sledge together without being kemmerings, as we say in Eskeve — eh?" Genly Ai, who will come to share a point of view with Estraven, speaks sometimes in aphorisms, even giving their Ekumenical source, but is not self-conscious about the need to gain wisdom from someone else's experience: "One voice speaking truth is a greater force than fleets and armies" and "As they say in Ekumenical School, when action grows unprofitable, gather information; when information grows unprofitable, sleep." Finally, having experienced enough himself, Genly Ai grows and this growth is reflected (determines) his speaking in aphorisms of his own invention: "It is good to have an end to journey towards; but it is the journey that matters, in the end." The use of aphorisms, apparently determined by the characters, in fact reflects the characteristics that Le Guin wills and wishes to communicate.

We work our way back through the logic of determinism to understand this narrative world as one of potential wisdom, and we work our way back through the logic of invention to understand this narrative world as serving an author's freely willed purpose. Both conclusions are subsumed by the concern for point of view. Point of view can determine how the world appears to someone: mad Argaven is "'a king, and does not see things rationally, but as a king.'" Although Estraven says this, he does not follow up his insight carefully enough. "'Mr. Ai, we've seen the same events with different eyes; I wrongly thought they'd seem the same to us.'" Le Guin, however, who has created both Estraven and his lapse, makes no such error herself; the entire novel is structured by an awareness of point of view.

The opening lines of the novel show this awareness: "Truth is a matter of the imagination . . . the facts seem to alter with an altered voice . . . yet none of them are false, and it is all one story." True to this word, the novel proceeds by presenting the story first in one voice and then in another, first from one point of view, then from another. The first chapter begins with an italicized document heading, *"From the Archives of Hain."* This heading includes the words, *"Report from Genly Ai."* We do not know who Genly Ai is at this moment, of course, but when we read the first roman-faced word of the novel, "I," we know that it is Genly Ai speaking. Since this is a first person narration, chapter 1 inevitably forces us into a sympathetic, even if only partial, sharing of Genly Ai's point of view. The second chapter begins with an italicized announcement that we are about to read a *"'hearth-tale'"* as told by an unknown narrator. We quickly switch our point of view to take on the perspective necessary to an understanding of this chapter. The third chapter begins without italics but with the word "I." The human mind loves to generalize an instance into a law; having seen a chapter beginning with "I" turn out to be narrated by Genly Ai, we are likely to assume that this chapter is narrated by him as well. But even if we are not so quick to fix things, the text fixes them for us within the first sentence:

> I slept late and spent the tail of the morning reading over my own notes on Palace etiquette and the observations on Gethenian psychology and manners made by my predecessors, the Investigators.

The fourth chapter is again announced in italics as a "story," and so when the fifth chapter begins without notice, we assume we are back to Genly Ai's narration. And we turn out to be correct. Le Guin is training us to accept our logic of inference and to generalize the laws determining the novel's structure. Thus, when the sixth chapter begins without announcement, we should assume that it is *not* Genly Ai. And when it quickly becomes apparent that this is a first person narration, we wonder who is speaking. The text quickly pacifies our curiosity: in the third line of the chapter the cook says "in my ear, 'Wake up, wake up, Lord Estraven.'" Our guesses about the laws determining the novel's structure have been correct, and the novel has rewarded us with confirmation. All of this is being done for two very important reasons. First, by making the novel itself an example of the truth altering with altered voices, residing in diverse points of view, the very narrative method forces us to accept the novel's opening aphoristic premises. But an equally important reason is much less general and is well worth discussing.

Although Le Guin presents the novel through two first person voices and intersperses a series of other narratives, of folk literature, Investigators' reports and so on, she arranges to have the novel, nonetheless, move continuously forward. Each chapter picks up some point of plot or thought from its predecessors and proceeds. There is only one exception to this: the mindspeaking episode. From the beginning of the story, Estraven has wanted to learn mindspeaking. The novel has been a record of misperception by Estraven of Genly Ai and by Genly Ai of Estraven. But finally, by chapter 16, having escaped Pulefen Farm together and struggled up onto the Gobrin Ice, the two principal characters begin to talk more forthrightly. In their tent, the place inside the blizzard, when Genly Ai explains that his visit to Gethen, because of travel in the trans-light speed NAFAL ship, has prevented him from ever seeing his parents again, Estraven realizes that Genly is as much an exile from his birthplace as is the so-called Traitor. They are mutual exiles. "'You for my sake—I for yours.'" In this chapter, narrated by Estraven, we have not only the isolation of the two together and their sharing of a common and arduous task but Estraven's narration of his kemmer. Since Genly is always male, Estraven becomes female; they feel very close to each other, but they keep that closeness spiritual. Chapter 17 is "An Orgota Creation Myth" wherein the world of people is the result of copulation between aboriginal brothers in a hut made of death, corpses, within the blizzard. And then in chapter 18, "On the Ice," we return to first person narration. It is in this chapter that Genly Ai covers the same ground Estraven had covered in chapter 16, both geographically and narratively. The chapter begins with this line: "Sometimes as I am falling asleep in a dark, quiet room." An alert reader already knows that Genly Ai must live through this adventure since he has made his presence as "editor" of these materials clear in footnotes. An even more alert reader will note that one of the brothers in the creation myth preceding this chapter runs off immediately after copulation, never to return. If that story bears on ours — and it must or Le Guin would not have willed it there — then it is determined that one character must leave, and since that cannot be Genly Ai it must be Estraven. Hence, this recollection from the future must be Genly's and the chapter is indeed in his voice. It too tells of the growing closeness between Genly Ai and Estraven and of the night of kemmer and finally, closeness of closeness, mindspeech. Estraven mindhears Genly speak his given name, Therem, with the voice of his dead brother and kemmering, Arek. As the only event which is covered twice, as the symptom of love, and as the demonstration of the coincidence of Genly and Therem's points of view, this is perhaps the crucial event of the plot. Chapter 19, "Homecoming," begins without italics, and though it begins with first person pronouns, they are not singular:

> In a dark windy weather we slogged along, trying to find en-
> couragement in the sighting of Esherhoth Crags, the first
> thing not ice or snow or sky that we had seen for seven weeks.

This could be either character speaking, of course, but since Genly Ai narrated chapter 18 and since the law determining this novel's structure calls for alternation of narrative voices, this must be Estraven speaking. And so we read this in our minds with Estraven's voice, and it fits, until a page goes by and then the speaker indicates that he knows his recollec-tion is correct "by Estraven's journal, for I kept none." The law is broken! And we have mindheard Genly with Therem's voice! By her consummate manipulation of point of view, Le Guin has given us the experience which her novel had described. Suddenly, we fully under-stand the mutuality of the characters' points of view and therefore under-stand the beauty of such loss of self. From the point of view of point of view, both determinism and free will seem insignificant. In the middle of the novel, the antagonism of determinism and free will is critical for Genly Ai; he ends chapter 8 with this thought about Estraven:

> It crossed my mind . . . that I had not come to Mishnory to
> eat roast blackfish with the Commensals of my own free will;
> nor had they brought me here. He had.

But after mindspeaking. their wills are one and the question of determinism is no longer relevant. In making us see this, Le Guin has used determinism

— of sex and of environment, of language and style and image and technique and structure — not to create a sense of free will but to subsume both determinism and free will under the recognition that "truth is a matter of the imagination."

As we saw in the characters' use of aphorisms, Genly Ai and Estraven begin the novel as apparently opposed and, although both learn, primarily Genly grows toward Estraven, the two finally coming to an understanding that does not so much reconcile their differences as make them irrelevant by acknowledging and accepting them as necessary for mutual fulfillment. In this regard, the central utterance of the novel is "Tormer's Lay":

> Light is the left hand of darkness
> and darkness the right hand of light.
> Two are one, life and death, lying
> together like lovers in kemmer
> like hands joined together,
> like the end and the way.

This is a part of the literature of the Handdara, the religion of which Estraven is an adept. Only after the mindspeaking does Genly seem to understand it fully and he offers to gloss it by drawing in Estraven's notebook the yin and yang symbol: "'Light, dark. Fear, courage. Cold, warmth. Female, male. . . . Both and one. A shadow on snow.'" In coming to understand the Handdara, Genly — and the reader — come to understand something of Chinese philosophy, and in particular of Taoism.

"To oppose something is to maintain it," Estraven notes in his typically aphoristic and paradoxical manner. Compare that with this from the *Tao Teh King* of Lao Tzu, the oldest document of Taoism: "In conflicts between opposites, the more one attacks his seeming opponent . . . the more he defeats himself." Not only does Taoism present its message in aphoristic paradox, it also uses anecdote in the ways of this novel. Chapter 4, "The Nineteenth Day," tells of a man who wanted to know the length of his life and foolishly asked the Handdarata Foretellers for the day of his death. He is told he will die on the nineteenth — but not of which month or year. This maddens him and to save his sanity his lover offers his own life to learn how long the man will live. He is told that he will live longer than the lover. When he reports this answer, the man becomes murderous because the lover wasted his question. He kills the lover and this so sobers and shocks him that the next month he hangs himself, on the nineteenth. In this parable the Fore-tellers indeed tell the truth: the lover pays for the prophecy with his life, the man outlives his lover and he dies on the nineteenth. But even though the Foretellers have the skill of predicting the future (which would imply that it is determined), they predict it for a reason of their own: "'To exhibit the perfect uselessness of knowing the answer to the wrong questions.'" Both the man and his lover would have been much better off to have acted in accord with the Tao, to have lived as long as they would live, and die when they would die. Then, even had they died on the same days, they would have been spared the madness, and per-haps have known peace. Compare that story with this from Chuang-tzu, the most famous interpreter of Tao:

> Hui Tzu said to Chuang-tzu, "Your teachings are of no prac-tical use." Chuang-tzu said, "Only those who already know the value of the useless can be talked to about the useful. This earth we walk upon is of vast extent, yet in order to walk a man uses no more of it than the soles of his two feet will cover. But suppose one cut away the ground round his feet till one reached the Yellow Springs [the land of the dead], would his patches of ground still be of any use to him for walking?" Hui Tzu said, "They would be of no use." Chuang-tzu said, "So then the usefulness of the useless is evident."

This story teaches that the useless is itself useful, and the Foretelling of the Handdara, although useless in changing the determined course of men's lives by allowing the consequential application of free will is useful in teaching men to live with ignorance. Whether a given parable, or the ground under a man's feet, is of value is a matter of point of view. Value, after all, depends upon the evaluator. To the Tao, sometimes called the Way and somtimes called Nature, all things are equally valuable and valueless because all things are equally true, equally part of the Tao.

In Taoism the best action is informed non-action, allowing people and things to act out their own natures. In ancient China Lao Tzu inter-preted the Tao in this way and drew from it not only conclusions about attitudes but even guides to right action in government. He saw the best governors as those who led the people to fulfill their own natures. This is Estraven's gift as well:

> I never had a gift but one, to know when the great wheel gives to a touch, to know and act . . . It was a delight to feel that

> certainty again, to know that I could steer my fortunes and the world's chance like a bobsled down the steep, dangerous hour.

One cannot help but note that according to legend, when Lao Tzu saw the dynasty about to decline he left and, before disappearing forever, gave his teachings to a gatekeeper. Therem too leaves Karhide when he sees that dynasty — and all dynasties — about to pass. The gate image of Taoism in this novel is seen as the arch image. The novel opens with the ceremony of Argaven setting the keystone to the arch of the bridge that will open the New Road. The mortar is red. Previously that color had come from human sacrifice; now from animals. Therem sees, at that very ceremony, that it is Genly Ai who will "'show us the new road.'" And, forming a narrative bridge itself, after Estraven's murder by Tibe's agents at the end of the book, Genly Ai returned

> through the Northern Gates to Erhenrang . . . it came plainly to me that, my friend being dead, I must accomplish the thing he died for. I must set the keystone in the arch.

Therem's blood will support this newer and more important bridge — and simultaneously bridge the novel. Things happen as they are to happen. That is the Way.

Chuang-tzu, who came well after Lao Tzu, tried neither to persuade nor advise. He tried to keep out of the affairs of men, preferring to concentrate on the liberating contemplation of the Tao. In this, he is much like Faxe the Weaver, another Handdara adept who understands the uselessness of knowing the answer to the wrong question and who, once Estraven has passed from the scene, must take his place. Chuang-tzu's main object of satire was Confucius because Confucius paid special attention to political problems. In his time,

> the efforts of . . . powerful families to transform the state into family domains conflicted with the desires of lesser nobles and wealthy citizens for a united state to be ruled by men according to their merits, education and character. The latter formed a relatively democratic movement, although it naturally excluded the working people, especially peasants, from government, relegating them to the role of beneficiaries of paternalistic care.

> The ideas of this group were fundamentally formulated by

Confucius, and his teachings were thus well suited to form the backbone of the bureaucratic state which developed in China.

The description of the Confucian nation, and its opposition of the organization by "domains," fits Gethen perfectly.

It had been entertaining and fascinating to find here on Gethen governments so similar to those in the ancient histories of Terra: a monarchy, and a genuine fullblown bureaucracy.

Although *The Left Hand of Darkness* clearly presents a world parallel to our own, in the matter of governments the parallel is not to our time but to the time of the legendary Chuang-tzu.

One ought not to conclude, of course, that Le Guin's novel is a simple *roman à clef.* There are crucial discrepancies between Chinese history and this narrative, an obvious example being the contemporaneity of Estraven and Faxe. The use of Chinese philosophy and literature as a source should not be taken too far. The Orgota creation myth, for example, that depends upon ice melt, seems much more closely aligned with the Norse creation myth than with anything in Chinese literature. Nonetheless, this novel seems clearly indebted to an ancient philosophy of dynamic opposition and active unity. "If Nature is inexpressible, he who desires to know Nature as it is in itself will not try to express it in words." Yet, this is what Lao Tzu did by writing this paradoxical aphorism and what Le Guin does by writing her book. In all novels the actions of characters are determined. After all, whatever will have happened to them by the time we have read the last page has already been written as having happened to them when we begin to read the first page. Yet, to become involved in the rightness or wrongness of their decisions, we must think of them as if they had free will. So, all characters are determined and all require us to adopt a point of view that sees them as free. In this book, that fact about narrative becomes a thematic concern, and the problem of determinism versus free will is set aside by turning to the notion of point of view. This is a matter of situating one's mind, a matter at the heart of Taoism.

In its use of paradox, aphorism, historical parallels, and particulars of philosophy, this novel seems to attempt to bring its readers around to sharing, experiencing, the Taoist point of view. According to that point of view, the Tao is whatever it is; things happen as they must. This is exemplified in the novel by the accuracy of the Foretellers. When Genly Ai asks them a sufficiently precise question about his mission, will Gethen join the Ekumen within five years, the answer is not at all paradoxical: "yes." One cannot help but wonder, then, if that implies that such an answer also is useless and that Genly Ai and Estraven might have saved themselves the trouble. But the answer to that is equally clear: they had to do what it appeared to their natures to do, that is the Tao way and the novel's point of view. "Intelligence consists in acting according to Nature." By acting out their natures, they accomplished the Taoist goal of coming to understand their own true natures and each other's. In this way, as the *Tao Teh King* asserts, they can guide the world they live in and finally bring other people's points of view into conformity with their own. The boundaries of nations crumble because these two could come to understand, mindspeak, each other. When in the last chapter Genly Ai goes to see Estraven's homeland and to offer what solace he can to his friend's relatives, Estraven's father wants to know about the journey across the ice, but his son, in whom Genly Ai sees "the flash of my friend's spirit," asks, "'Will you tell us how he died? — Will you tell us about the other worlds out among the stars — the other kinds of men, the other lives?" "It is natural for man to be born and to die." Therem and his son both know this, and both are ready for the great adventure, into death and into the stars, an adventure of the body, to be sure, but much more an adventure of the mind. Mankind's perpetual struggle has been to change the world, to understand how it is determined and to impose human will upon it. According to the Tao and according to Le Guin's novel, this struggle ceases, and peace and liberation follow, when a person holds to and accepts the Nature of things. What one needs to expand one's mind, to gain flexibility in adapting one's own point of view to the nature of the people and things around one, to learn to see people not as men and women but as people, to see the world for what it really is and for what it really does to us, to understand the languages of mankind as the reflections of mankind, to see that all things fit, as in a novel, into a pattern. And to be open to seeing more of the pattern. To come to this understanding is not useless at all, but neither is it the answer to a question spoken by a character. This is not an answer in the novel; it is the novel.

The Left Hand of Darkness: Androgyny, Future, Present, and Past

Barbara Brown

Much of the impact of Ursula K. Le Guin's *The Left Hand of Darkness* (1969) results from the fact that the novel is an exploration of the concept of the dichotomous/androgynous one on three time levels: future, present, and past. First and most obviously, it is future directed, presenting a possible androgynous world on the planet Winter. Second, it is rooted in the present. As Le Guin affirms in her introduction to the Ace edition, the purpose of her science fiction is descriptive, not predictive: "I'm merely observing, in the peculiar, devious, and thought-experimental manner proper to science fiction, that if you look at us at certain odd times of the day . . . we already are [androgynous]." Third, *The Left Hand of Darkness* is directed to the past. In her exploration of androgyny, Le Guin examines a subject whose origins are buried deep in our mythic past.

The term androgyny, itself, reflects the past, present, and future orientation of the novel. Increasingly, we hear the word used in the present by writers like Carolyn Heilbrun in *Toward a Recognition of Androgyny* and June Singer in *Androgyny*. They, and other sociologists, use the term to describe a present theory of human sexuality that will provide a viable future pattern for psychological and cultural evolution if we can synthesize the ancient, past knowledge of our androgynous beginnings with our contemporary experiences.

The very origins of the word, lying in our past, in ancient Greece suggest a beginning definition. Androgyny is a combination of *andro* meaning male and *gyn* meaning female. It suggests by its form a blending

From *Extrapolation* 21, no. 3 (Fall 1980).©1980 by the Kent State University Press.

in which human characteristics of males and females are not rigidly assigned. One might simply assert then that the androgyne is the dichotomous one, imcorporating male and female psychological duality in one physical entity. There are, though, more complex ideas currently associated with the word. Androgyny is an affirmation that humanity should reject all forms of sexual polarization, emerge from the prison of gender into a world in which individual behavior can and is freely chosen.

We need a word of caution here. Androgyny is not a prescription for blandness, for homogeneity, for the submerging of differences. Human experience will always be paradoxical, containing opposite energies and qualities. According to Jungians, the life system works as a result of the dynamics of the interaction of the opposites. We must have this tension. In androgyny, however, the source of the dynamics is not the opposition of male and female but rather alternating thrust and withdrawal of the masculine and feminine principles within each individual psyche.

In practical terms, then, the theory of androgyny affirms that we should develop a mature sexuality in which an open system of all possible behavior is accepted, the temperament of the individual and the surrounding circumstances being the determining factors, rather than gender. In some aspects androgyny involves the reacquisition of what Freud defines as the polymorphously perverse body of the child. In this situation the individual considers every area, not just the genital, as potentially erogenous. He or she develops beyond gender limitation.

The preceding interpretation of androgyny in the present is certainly part of what concerns Le Guin. However, her presentation of the androgynous beings in *The Left Hand of Darkness* also encompasses the original archetypes. These archetypes express the underlying human conviction that man had once experienced a unity that is now denied by the basic division into male and female. Any review of the creation myths reveals an astounding number of androgynous situations. June Singer in her excellent study of the subject includes a detailed analysis of these creation stories. Some of the more obvious examples are briefly referred to here. Consider that the Bible includes two versions of creation. In Genesis, chapter 1, it is an androgynous God who creates both man and woman in his image. In the second version in Genesis, it is the hermaphroditic Adam who produces Eve from his side. The patriarchal Jewish society emphasized this latter version.

Both the early Gnostic writings and Kabalistic literature present pictures of the androgynous origins of man. Traditional pictures of Adam Kadmon, the first man, according to Kabalists, show the genitals combining male and female organs. Eventually, as this complicated myth develops, primal man is torn apart and male and female become opposites.

There is also an androgynous version of creation in Plato's *Symposium:* "[The] original human nature was not like the present, but different. The sexes were not two, as they are now, but originally three in number; there was man, woman and a union of the two, having a name corresponding to this double nature, which once had a real existence, but is now lost, and the word 'Androgynous' is only preserved as a term of reproach." As this creation story unfolds the gods are attacked by this unified creature. The punishment for its defiance is division into the two parts of man, male and female. Each part them continues to desire the other half, trying to gain completion.

Similarly, this concept of the paradoxical, split yet unified, male and female principle is found in Chinese mythology. This traditional belief is embodied in the *I Ching* or *Book of Changes* dated sometime between 2000 to 1300 B.C. Here the supreme ultimate generates the primary forms, the Yin and the Yang. All nature then consists of a perpetual interplay between this primordial pair. They are Yang and Yin, heat and cold, fire and water, active and passive, masculine and feminine.

While Le Guin works out of this mythic/religious background, she also continues "the hidden river of androgyny" in literature so well discussed in Carolyn Heilbrun's book *Toward a Recognition of Androgyny.* One might interpret the triumph of Orestes and Athena in the *Oresteia* as the union of the male and female dualities. Later, the deification of the Virgin Mary in the medieval period balances the principle of the deified masculine in God. There are androgynous women throughout Shakespeare. They choose to defy social conditioning and assert masculine temperaments: the ambitious Lady MacBeth, the sexually determined Desdemona, the lustful Goneril and Regan. Moll Flanders in Defoe's eighteenth-century novel is an androgynous figure in her defiance of the traditionally passive role assigned to women of the time as is Hester Prynne in *The Scarlet Letter* and Nora in *A Doll's House.* Consider *Orlando* by Virginia Woolf. Here Woolf makes explicit the androgyny she so favors in the concluding chapters of *A Room of One's Own.* For a real life account of androgyny read Jan Morris' *Conundrum.* This androgynous passage in Herman Hesse's *Siddhartha* confirms how a conviction of the androgynous potential for man appears in unexpected places. When Siddhartha dreams of meeting his friend Govinda:

> He dreamt that Govinda stood before him, in the yellow robe of the ascetic. Govinda looked sad and asked him, "Why did you leave me?" Thereupon he embraced Govinda, put his arm round him, and as he drew him to his breast and kissed him, he was Govinda no longer, but a woman and out of the woman's gown emerged a full breast and Siddhartha lay there and drank . . . it tasted of woman and man, of sun and forest, of animal and flower.

According to the perceptions of many writers, we are, indeed, male and female. This recognition of androgyny as our ideal is buried in our mythology, in our literature, in our subconscious, and in our cells. Ursula Le Guin draws upon this past tradition of the mythic and literary androgyne and her recognition of the androgynous behavior in our present society when she writes her future-based novel, *The Left Hand of Darkness.*

Le Guin is aware how difficult her readers will find acceptance of the androgynous principle. To make explicit the need for such a non-Western interpretation of experience, she first establishes the movement from duality to unity on all levels of Genly Ai's experience, then depicts his increasing sensitivity to the peripheral ambiguities of truth that contradict the central facts.

We begin with duality into unity in terms of imagery, setting, characters, action, and philosophy. Traditionally, the right side has been associated with light representing knowledge, rationality, and the male principle; the left with darkness, ignorance, and the female principle. In *The Left Hand of Darkness* the initial description of the setting immediately establishes this light/dark, left/right polarity. The novel opens with "Rain clouds over dark towers . . . a dark storm-beaten city." Yet there is one vein of slowly winding gold. This is the parade. Genly, the protagonist, sees these as contrasts, separate facets of the scene. They are, though, part of one unified vision of the world of Winter.

The wider universe is depicted in terms of light and dark. The mad Argaven, King of Karhide, mentions that the stars are bright and blinding, providing a traditional account of the universe. Continuing the description, he expands it, insisting on the surrounding void, the terror and the darkness that counterpoint the rational light of the interplanetary alliance of the Ekumen that Genly symbolizes. The glacier, the heart of Winter, is so bright on the Gobrin Ice it almost blinds Genly and his travelling companion, Estraven, the proscribed first minister of Karhide. Yet is is dark and terrible when they are caught between Drumner and Dremegole, the volcanos, spewing out black smoke and ash.

The action in the novel is often described in terms of dualities. At Arikostor Fastness, Genly specifically mentions the thin strips of light that creep across the circle. They are counterpoints of the slats of dimness. The weaver, Faxe, a man, is seen as a woman dressed in light in the center of darkness. The foretellers are a part of a bright spider web, light against dark.

Toward the conclusion of his journey, both Genly and the reader perceive the merging pattern of dualities on these levels of setting and action. Light and dark, left and right, and, by implication, male and female become whole. Estraven quotes "Tormer's Lay" to Genly:

> Light is the left hand of darkness
> and darkness the right hand of light.
> Two are one, life and death, lying
> together like lovers in kemmer,
> like hands joined together,
> like the end and the way.

Genly and Estraven yearn for the dark of the shadow when they are in the antarctic void of the white darkness. Without shadow, without dark, there is a surfeit of light. They cannot see ahead to avoid the threatening changes in the terrain. In total understanding, Genly draws for Estraven the Yang and the Yin, the light and the dark. "Both and one," he says; "A shadow on snow." Both are necessary. Ultimately, Genly recognizes their crossing of the ice is both success and failure: union with the Ekumen, death for Estraven. Both are necessary.

But light and dark, left and right are not the only polarities that are unified as preparatory patterns for the central sexual unification. There is political duality in the opposed states of Orgoreyn and Karhide. Karhide has a slow steady pace of change. In many ways it is disunited. While it speaks to the people's sense of humanity, fostering a sense of strong individualism and family loyalty based on the conception of the hearths, like many democracies it harbors within it the possibility of the rise of fascism and susceptibility to demagogues.

Orgoreyn is more socialist. Burdened down by the rivalries of its Commensalities, the extensiveness of its bureaucracies, the pettiness of its inspectors, it nonetheless is ordered and unified. It conveys a sense of progress. Still, it terrifies Genly with its failure to respect the rights of the individual. These political polarities exist not only between the two states but also within each, since the individual systems are at the same time both rational and irrational.

Genly, disgusted with this ambiguity, embraces Karhide, then rejects it; accepts Orgota, then flees from it. He seeks a consistent rational pattern. There is none. This is precisely Le Guin's thesis. Ambiguous duality must exist if unification is to occur.

This state of political polarity is unified by the agency of the Ekumen. Not a kingdom but a coordinator, it serves as a clearinghouse for trade and knowledge for the eighty-three nations within its scope. Mystical in nature, the Ekumen works slowly, seeking consensus. Estraven immediately recognizes that the Ekumen is a greater weaver than the Handdara. It has woven all aliens into one fabric that reflects both the unity and diversity of the civilized world.

This pattern of unifying dualities is clearly related to the central concern of androgyny. Without an awareness of the possibility of unifying opposites on the imaginative, physical, and political levels, we would not be as willing to alter the present sexual dichotomy we experience. According to Ursula Le Guin, at times we already perceive the androgynous possibilities within us. She suggests we are, nonetheless, unable to explore fully this unified duality. One reason for this limitation is the restrictive way the Western mind interprets human experience. (A similar view is promulgated by Taoism and Zen.) This linear approach, characterizing Western thought, focuses on scientifically provable facts. As a result it is narrow and exclusive. It fails to incorporate our peripheral senses which, through intuition and mystical awareness, also contribute to knowledge. Through the action in *The Left Hand of Darkness,* Le Guin suggests that by utilizing this peripheral vision we, like Genly, can learn to accept life with all its ambiguities, its paradoxes, its flow, its unknowable qualities, with all its androgyny.

At the beginning of *The Left Hand of Darkness,* Genly is limited by the Western mode of thought. As a scientist observing a subject, there is a tacit assumption of superiority on his part. He admits early in the first chapter that he judges the Gethenians as aliens. His detached manner leads him mistakenly to assert that the rivalry between Tibe, the traitorous cousin of the King, and Estraven is irrelevent to his cause. He dislikes Estraven because he is obscure, not an easy subject for scientific research. Notably, Genly's poor judgment of Winter's cultures results from his desire to gather the facts and proceed to logical conclusions. He is skeptical of anything that cannot be labeled and categorized.

Only by abandoning his devisive scientific approach can Genly achieve the unification of the warring philosophical and sexual elements within him. First, however, there are many ambiguities he must accept. One of these is Shifgrethor, an ambiguous conveying of information and intent. Not lying, it is a viable mode of behavior, conveying one aspect of truth. The wheel of experience, as Estraven insists, is not factually knowable. It turns independent of human control. On the Gobrin Ice, Genly must accept this ambiguity. No one can predict his success or failure on the glacier. As well, Genly eventually perceives that opposites are not exclusive, not contradictory. Estraven is both patriot and traitor. Genly is both patriot and traitor. Loyal to his mission, he brings Winter into the Ekumen; yet he betrays Estraven by permitting the landing of the starship before forcing Argaven to recall Therem's condemnation. Life is not linear as Genly first believes. Since it is process, the Gethenian system of measuring time is not alien but rather a logical emphasis of the individual's perception as the center of meaningful experience.

Finally, Genly accepts the ambiguous flow of events that makes it an impossibility to contain truth in language. In discussing Therem's behavior with Argaven, he says, "As I spoke I did not know if what I said was true. True in part; an aspect of truth." Often it is the West that affirms that there is one truth that can be logically explicated. It is the East that perceives that truth is flowing and ebbing, inexplicably diffuse, androgynous.

Ironically, this recognition of the many facets of truth is revealed in the beginning of *The Left Hand of Darkness*. Here the enlightened Genly, now looking back with wisdom on his experiences on Winter, declares that truth is a matter of the imagination (Eastern) but one can write a report on events (Western) containing facts (Western). However, those facts, since they are neither solid nor coherent, will glow or dull according to the speaker (Eastern).

The unification of all these dualities, the acceptance of these ambiguities, prepares both Genly and the reader to accept the central thematic unity of the sexual hermaphroditism of the Gethenians. In his response to the aliens, Genly reveals what Le Guin assumes the reader's feelings might be to these dichotomous characters. Estraven is first described as "the person on my left." Appropriately he is involved in feminine intrigue; however, he is wearing green, gold, and silver. These are colors not usually associated with both the right (the masculine) and with the left (the feminine). By page 122 Estraven is on Genly's right, all male now, but defying the traditional symbolism of right and left, he is a dark, shadowy figure. Associated with both light and dark, with left and right in a deliberately reversed symbolic order, Estraven is also an ambiguous figure. Neither Genly Ai nor the reader can interpret such a character according to traditional concepts. This world of Winter denies the established polarities of the light and dark, left and right, male and female.

Initially, the mobile responds to this confusion on the basis of his cultural conditioning. While he is repelled by the sexual duality of the Karhiders, he can neither overtly reveal his feelings to his hosts nor covertly admit his distaste to himself. His language, his responses, though, record his uneasiness. Genly first describes Estraven in these revealing terms declaring he was "Annoyed by [his] sense of effeminate intrigue." Later he calls Estraven a strange alien. He is oblivious to the fact that Estraven is the Karhider who has most attempted to befriend him. In a patronizing manner, Genly mentions that his landlady seems male on first meeting but also has "fat buttocks that wagged as he walked and a soft fat face, and a prying, spying ignoble, kindly nature. . . . He was so feminine." In commenting on the lack of war on Gethen, Genly observes, "They lacked, it seemed, the capacity to mobilize. They behaved like animals, in that respect; or like women. They did not behave like men or ants." Finally, in describing Therem in their relationship, he affirms, "There was in his attitude something feminine, a refusal of the abstract, the ideal, a submissiveness to the given which displeased me."

At the beginning of *The Left Hand of Darkness,* Genly divides these unified creatures into polarities. He perceives the Gethenians in single bodies responding as both male and female. This merging of the stereotyped roles and responses first shocks and then revolts him.

The completion of his mission, however, brings him to full understanding of the nature of all dualities. They are extremes on a continuum, separated but nonetheless joined, unified. Duality can be unity. Genly must accept this fact and find ease in it. For him the crossing on the ice is a journey to self and universal knowledge. Genly begins by sharing supplies with Estraven; moves to encompassing him with mindspeak; concludes by totally accepting Estraven's nature and, by extension, the androgyny of his own. Toward the conclusion of their journey, Genly admits,

> What I was left with was, at last, acceptance of him as he was.
> Until then I had rejected him, refused him his own reality.

He had been quite right to say that he, the only person on Gethen who trusted me, was the only Gethenian I distrusted. For he was the only one who had entirely accepted me as a human being; who had liked me personally and given me entire personal loyalty, and who therefore had demanded of me an equal degree of recognition, of acceptance. I had not been willing to give it. I had been afraid to give it. I had not wanted to give my trust, my friendship to a man who was a woman, a woman who was a man.

By later drawing the symbol of the Yang and Yin, light and dark, masculine and feminine, Genly makes visible his emotional and intellectual acceptance of Estraven: the two in the one.

Le Guin, however, does not conclude with Genly's recognition of the androgynous possibility. Her ending suggests that this state of unified duality is a preferable, superior state of existence. In the final chapter, Genly no longer relates to his own species nor they to him. He is alien to the Terran arrivals. Uneasy in his new perceptions, Genly calls the representatives of the Ekumen "a troupe of great, strange animals of two different species, great apes with intelligent eyes, all of them in rut, in kemmer." He is happy to return to the company of the young Gethenian physician who is described in these terms: "and his face, a young serious face, not a man's face and not a woman's, a human face, these were a relief to me, familiar, right."

In *The Left Hand of Darkness* Ursula Le Guin suggests we too should accept as right, as familiar, the archetypal androgyny within us. Transcending male, transcending female, we can become fully human.

Conversational Technique in Ursula Le Guin: A Speech-Act Analysis

Victoria Myers

It is apparently impossible to translate affection or trust, friendship or love into the special language of secrecy and indirection used by the diplomatic milieu of Gethen in Ursula K. Le Guin's *The Left Hand of Darkness* (*LHD*). Yet Genly Ai and Estraven, though belonging to different planets, do create the bonds of friendship and love using this very language. This paradox hints at Le Guin's solution to the perennial dilemma facing the SF writer: she must create aliens convincingly different from us to challenge our sympathetic imagination, but she must also give us the means to eventually understand them. Le Guin sees the task as among other things a linguistic one: how to create a language for the alien. The problem as she interprets it is really two-fold: (1) establishing the "otherness" of the language, so as to erect convincing barriers to communication between the alien and the earthling and to do this even though, in fact, the language she writes in must be predominantly the language of the audience; and (2) achieving a sense of ordeal — a sense of gradual growth and enlightenment — in overcoming the barriers to communication.

She obviously accomplishes the first of these two objectives by introducing certain "untranslatable" terms from the alien language into the language in which the Envoy makes his report, terms such as *kemmer* and *shifgrethor* and the various words for snow. But she accomplishes both the estrangement and the familiarization in a more subtle way as well: by manipulating the conditions and elements of speech acts.

From *Science-Fiction Studies* 10, no. 3 (November 1983). ©1983 by SFS Publications.

Without violating our accustomed procedures for understanding language or having to invent "rules" for our perception of conversation, Le Guin characterizes communication with the alien by manipulating the intrinsic structures of ordinary conversation. To describe her technique, I shall adapt from the speech-act theories of J. L. Austin and J. R. Searle some useful concepts pertaining to liguistic description.

I

It is perhaps somewhat risky to offer a linguistic approach to fiction.

Even though this has been done before, it has met with considerable hostility, and on admittedly good grounds. Linguistics concentrates not on written language, and certainly not on the literary use of language, but rather on speech, on everyday discourse. Yet I do not think that we find an unbreachable wall between literature and the everyday uses of language. For one thing, the minute we try to describe everyday language, we find we are crossing over into literature by way of metaphor, irony, and other non-literal but common uses of language. For another, even literal utterances in fictional speech acts are to all appearances indistinguishable from their real-life counterparts. Of course, as Searle himself recognizes, speech acts in fiction do not have the same force as those in life; we do not expect a fictional promise to be fulfilled in the real world. Yet fictional speech acts are parallel to or parasitical on nonliterary ones in so far as they pretend to be like them. A promise from one fictional character to another, we believe, sets up the expectation that it will be fulfilled in the world of the novel. In a work that attempts to be mimetic, therefore, speech-act theory can account for the conversation of the characters in the way it would the language of real life.

In order to get a feel for what precisely needs accounting for, let us look at a scene near the beginning of *LHD,* Genly Ai's short *tête-à-tête* with Lord Tibe, the nephew of the King. Probably the most important thing about this scene is that Genly does understand that Tibe's conversation with him about Estraven contains double meanings. When Tibe says cunningly: "Indeed, Lord Estraven is famous for his kindness to foreigners," Genly can sense that Tibe accuses Estraven of disloyalty to his own country. Of course, Genly has been in Karhide for a year, so he should be familiar with the Karhidish language and at least the outlines of the Karhiders' cultural assumptions. But, if this is true, then why does he not understand the indirect advice Tibe gives him a little later in this scene? Tibe's advice occurs in this form: "Ah yes! I keep forgetting that you come from another planet. But of course that's not a matter you ever forget. Though no doubt life would be much sounder and simpler and safer for you here in Ehrenrang if you could forget, eh?" His advice is phrased as a question, but he does not really expect, or even wait for, an answer. This fact is the listener's immediate clue that Tibe does not ask a sincere question. He does, however, explicitly state one of the necessary conditions for the giving of advice, that is, that Genly Ai would *benefit* by the predicated act. The actual advice is veiled in the conditional "would." Genly could easily perceive that Tibe was not sincerely questioning, and he may also perceive the act as advice; but he lacks that piece of information about Tibe's attitude toward himself to really understand the *nature* of Tibe's advice. Genly is prevented from full comprehension by his inability to see Tibe's intended meaning behind "foreigners" in the first remark of Tibe's cited. When he comments that "Few foreigners are so foreign as I, Lord Tibe," he assumes that Tibe recalls his having come from Earth. Tibe, as it later emerges, does not have this in mind at all: he sees Genly Ai as a Gethenian pervert, perhaps as an agent of Karhide's enemy, Orgoreyn. Thus, Genly would be able to see no danger in his representing himself to be what he in fact is — an Envoy of the Ekumen. Thus also, though the indirect form of the advice would be clear to him, the content would not be.

To the question posed earlier — why Genly does not understand Tibe's indirect advice — the obvious answer is that Genly lacks some vital piece of information about the political situation in Karhide: namely, Tibe's imminent rise to power and his opposition to Genly as Estraven's protegé. That this is the obvious answer should give us pause. It means that Genly Ai, and the reader along with him, knows how to decode not only the literal but also the non-literal utterances of Karhide; it implies that information and cultural assumptions have the same way of finding their way into language on Gethen as they have on Earth. It also means that Genly Ai will succeed or fail in understanding communications in Karhidish for the same reasons and in the same way that he would in his own Earth language. The source of otherness in the language of the aliens will come from the same things that cause misunderstanding or deceit in daily discourse.

Speech-act theory lends itself to a discussion of these transactions between self and "other," in that it attempts to account in a formal way for the *possibility* of communication. In the partial analysis just given, I have already used some of the terms of speech-act analysis. Let me explain those terms and the premises they arise from. According to Searle, "On the speaker's side, saying something and meaning it are closely connected with *intending* to produce certain effects on the hearer. On the hearer's side, understanding the speaker's utterance is closely connected with recognizing his *intentions*. In the case of literal utterances, the bridge between the speaker's side and the hearer's side is provided by their common language." More is meant by "their common language" than simply getting the hearer to decode the speaker's syntax. Some place must also be found for the physical and cultural context of the speech act, for the mental and emotional condition of the speaker and hearer, for these help to determine the speaker's intentions, and hence knowledge of them helps the listener to interpret those intentions, both in cases of literal utterances and of nonliteral utterances.

Searle (expanding on certain definitions ventured by Austin) has shown that utterances convey something more than "propositional content" (i.e., content that can be verified simply as true or false). Utterances containing virtually identical propositions carry different *illocutionary force;* that is, they have a different relationship to the world of action or to the psychological state of the speaker. An utterance predicating "crossing the street" of "George" can, for example, carry the force of an assertion or an order — "George is crossing the street," as compared with "George, cross the street." Thus the speaker performs a different act and intends a different effect on the hearer by each of these utterances.

Although illocutionary force may in part be analyzed by means of conventional syntactic and dictional signals, it is more precisely understood in terms of criteria called "felicity conditions," which necessitate consideration of the mental states of speaker and hearer. If, for example, I wished to give advice (an extremely important type of speech act in *LHD*), I could not successfully do so unless: (1) I proposed some future act of my hearer (this is merely the propositional condition, the necessary syntax); (2) I believed the act would benefit my hearer (the sincerity condition); (3) it was not obvious to either of us that my hearer would, without prompting, do this act (the preparatory condition). If, for instance, I did not believe the act would benefit my hearer, my act would not actually constitute advice, but some other kind of speech act.

If each of these conditions could be specified further, they would indicate what clues in the verbal and physical context would tell the hearer that, for example, the speaker is sincere in offering advice, that in fact what he or she is offering is advice and not warning or threat. Speech-act theory cannot presently do this; and given the complexity, even idiosyncrasy, of the information encoded on each occasion, it may never be able to do this. Still, in a sense, these conditions constitute the interstices of language, showing us how knowledge of events, of culture, even of self, makes its way into the communication process. This is especially evident in the theory's description of efforts at circuitous and polite communication like Tibe's indirect speech acts.

In indirect speech acts, often the syntax associated with one kind of illocutionary force is used to convey a different illocutionary force. For example, "Can you reach the salt?" is commonly understood not as a *question* about one's ability, but as a *request* for the salt. Searle shows that indirect speech acts are structurally related to their counterparts in that one can communicate the act by asking about one of the conditions or (often) stating that the condition is fulfilled. A preparatory condition for my requesting the salt from someone is the fact that it is within her or his power to give me the salt. Obviously, this could be understood only among speakers of a common dialect, sharers of common verbal assumptions. After all, one could ask for the salt, indirectly, in a multitude of ways. In some communities, it is conceivable that I could politely ask for the salt by asserting: "I know you don't like salt." This apparently factual statement might be construed as the preparatory condition for any request. We might go so far as to say that this way of asking for something suggests certain culturally held values, such as not asking for something that someone else likes. Certainly neither Austin nor Searle goes so far as to assign such values to specific concatenations of diction and syntax, nor can we legitimately do so *within* their theory. But I think that their theory does point to the places within the language where values make their appearance, and it suggests how they make their appearance.

It is precisely at the juncture where Tibe gives Genly advice that Genly has access to Tibe's values. Tibe praises Genly Ai's professed gratitude to Estraven ironically, telling him that this is a "noble" emotion, but rare in Ehrenrang — "no doubt because it's impracticable." Without overtly espousing it, he shows Genly a criterion for behavior (practicability) different from gratitude; and, though he would seem to favor gratitude, given his remark that a lack of it has made this "a hard age," we cannot at first be sure that Tibe is not one of those who accommodate themselves very well to things as they are. That Tibe embraces rather than opposes the criterion of practicability is a bit clearer in his indirect advice to Genly. It contains specifications (soundless, simplicity, safety) which are very much in the camp of practicability. All three of these derive from fear of the other. Soundness is the opposite of perversion, or of what appears to Tibe as perversion, a different organization of sexuality; simplicity is the opposite of complexity, the goal of the Ekumen; and safety, the opposite of adventure, of seeking the unknown and attempting to incorporate it into one's being. If, by means of conventional conversational signals, Genly Ai could ascertain that Tibe was not asking a question but giving advice, he could also have ascertained Tibe's criterion and taken it seriously. Le Guin will build on this linguistic fact to show that Genly must have understood the specifications of this criterion, and should have realized that as they oppose all that the Ekumen and he himself represent, Tibe consequently must be his foe. Relying on the implicit signals of normal speech, she will show in a later scene that, contrary to what we expect, Genly has accepted Tibe's values with no sense of their alienness.

Cultural and personal values enter the speech act in still another way. As a first step in interpreting an utterance, one participant must assume that the other is being cooperative, at least to the extent that she or he is attempting to communicate something or is replying to something just said. If the listener notes a discrepancy between what the speaker says and the immediate verbal or physical context, that listener assumes that he or she must interpret the speech act as non-literal or indirect. Suppose the following interchange: my husband and I are sitting in a room where the window is open. I say, "It's cold in here." He could easily interpret this as an indirect request to close the window. He says, "What's for supper?" Either he has not heard me, or he is refusing my request. It should be clear from this brief interchange that not only must the participants implicitly understand the rules for conveying indirect speech acts and have access to a certain informational context; they must also have a willingness to interpret along the lines indicated by these rules and context.

Recognition of this necessity is what, I think, prompted Austin to make a distinction between illocutionary force and *perlocutionary effect* (the action or attitude effected in the listener by means of the speech act). Just as every speech act usually has a propositional content, every speech act also has both illocutionary force and perlocutionary effect. The difference is ascertainable in the performative verbs we would use to describe the act in each case: "he advised me" would describe the illocutionary force, whereas "he persuaded me" might describe the perlocutionary effect of the same utterance. Austin points out that illocutionary force is always conveyed by conventional means, not only syntax and certain set dictional signals, but also conventional appurtenances in the environment; for example, only the duly constituted person can perform the marriage ceremony. The perlocutionary effect, on the other hand, is conveyed by means of the illocutionary force, but it may not be determined by it: the same speech act may have a different effect on different hearers or on the same hearer given different contexts.

When we speak of the hearer's *understanding* the speaker's intention, therefore, we must speak of two kinds of intention: (1) that which is the *sine qua non* of the communication itself, the intention of the speaker to communicate the propositional content and illocutionary force (e.g., to communicate advice as opposed to warning), and (2) the intention to have a certain effect on the hearer or to make him or her do something.

This distinction between illocutionary force and perlocutionary effect points to an important discrepancy in Genly Ai's behavior. We should expect him to find communication with Tibe more difficult than communication with Lord Estraven, who is Genly's friend and protector. But just the opposite is the case. The speech-act theory we have rehearsed so far will show that it is not so much Estraven's use of indirection which confuses the Envoy (though that is Genly's claim), but rather Genly's own refusal to cooperate in interpreting Estraven's indirect speech acts. We can see this refusal operating in the dinner scene between Genly and Estraven; it occurs immediately following the *tête-à-tête* with Tibe.

Estraven's conversation with Genly has no more indirection than Tibe's speech, although there is more grace and wit in Estraven's communications, and certainly different purport and different implied values. Estraven's indirections are polite ways of confessing his inability to help Genly further, of confessing his fall from power. He simultaneously protects himself from receiving condolences and preserves Genly from the embarrassment of hearing complaints and weakness, when he says in form of apology, "I'm sorry . . . that I've had to forestall for so long this pleasure of having you in my house; and to that extent at least I'm glad there is no longer any question of patronage between us." This is evidently Estraven's way of confirming the import of his inviting Genly to dinner; that is, as long as he was acting as Genly's patron, he could not show his personal favor by an invitation to dinner. His apology is not ironic (he does not mean the opposite of what he says), but the information is indirect (he means the apology, but he means something more as well).

Genly does not understand Estraven's refusal of further help, but only because he lacks that same bit of political *information* that lay behind Tibe's advice, not because he lacks the same *standards* of behavior that guide Estraven. Yet he thinks the latter is the cause of his confusion. When Estraven explains his inability to help Genly, with the question, "Did you hear what the king said to me at the ceremony today?" he sets Genly up to participate in a witty exchange: "'The king didn't speak to you in my hearing.' 'Nor in mine,' said he." The interpretation does not depend upon assumptions different from Genly's own supposed criteria. And Genly's participation in the elaborate witticism may be seen as simultaneously a way of making a joke at Estraven's expense, thereby defusing Genly's anger and disappointment, and of bringing the two people into harmony. This manipulation of words bespeaks Estraven's efforts at a "we-feeling" that Genly evidently does not share; he resents the joke as "effeminate deviousness" — almost as if he saw himself and not Estraven as the butt.

Genly Ai does co-operate in the speech transaction so far as to interpret indirect speech acts; and thus he receives the information Estraven wishes to transmit to him. But he judges the indirection and the information as if they were duplicitous, a persuasion which seems to override the clear signals of meaning in Estraven's speech. For example, after Estraven has been as plain as possible (relying almost soley on direct assertions), explaining that he has made trouble for himself in his attempt to eliminate the border dispute by aiding Karhidish farmers to move out of the Sinoth Valley and thereby offending the king, Genly comments to himself: "His ironies, and these ins and outs of a border-dispute with Orgoreyn, were of no interest to me. I returned to the matter that lay between us. Trust him or not, I might still get some use out of him." The reader should note, first, that Estraven has, immediately before this reflection, *not* been using irony, and second, that the tendency of this reflection constitutes part of a pattern, in which Genly, viewing himself as an emissary of the Ekumen (a messenger-boy) does not get personally involved in the mere political intrigues of Gethen, but at the same time reacts to Estraven's actions as if they regarded him personally. After Estraven has explained to Genly the reasons for the king's reaction to the offer of alliance with the Ekumen, Genly becomes introspective, contemplating his aloneness on this world and his vulnerability to Estraven, with whom he is at this moment apparently entirely alone; he loses belief in himself. As if in answer to these thoughts, Estraven says, "I believe you." It seems to foreshadow their communication in mind-speech, so close is the utterance to the thought. Still, Genly's reaction to this coincidence is not gratitude or even reciprocal belief, but bewilderment. Here he knows the relevant context; he even recites it to himself: Estraven has been the only person on this world to help him, has in fact effected a reversal in the way the Envoy is viewed. Yet Genly has never trusted him and finds in the present conversation only confirmation for his distrust.

Certainly Estraven at times speaks in ironies and double meanings; but these show us a person very different from Lord Tibe, who supports the philosophy of self-interest. Estraven tells Genly ironically that his actions in the Sinoth Valley were "not a patriotic idea. In fact it's a cowardly one, and impugns the shifgrethor of the king himself." But later, unlike Tibe, he explains his irony: "No, I don't mean love, when I say patriotism. I mean fear. The fear of the other." And: "I'm not acting patriotically. There are, after all, other nations on Gethen." Estraven, more directly than Tibe, tells Genly Ai what his criteria for political behavior are; in fact, they are the same nonnationalistic criteria one would presume guide Genly Ai in his mission from the Ekumen. But Genly interprets the indirect advice that he should take his offer to Orgoreyn (and he does not misunderstand the literal meaning of the advice) as a manifestation that Estraven is totally without loyalty. He ignores the fact that Estraven shares his supposed view of patriotism as a love of country which is compatible with trust in the other. Genly, without self-awareness, applies Tibe's criteria, interpreting Estraven's utterances as those of a traitor to the king, of someone devoid of loyalties to anyone. Genly uses Tibe's criteria because he does fear the other; he is so entrenched in the gender mentality of his world that he interprets Estraven's integral actions (his combination of charm and power) as expressions of duality, duplicity, "effeminate deviousness." In short, Genly Ai has (should have) knowledge of precisely the correct assumptions for judging Estraven's ironic statements, but he refuses to use them. Instead he interprets through the same assumptions as Tibe and the king — fear of the alien.

II

What I have said thus far should give some indication of how Le Guin performs the first task indicated for an SF writer — namely, making the audience aware of the barriers between themselves and the alien. That is, she shows that the Gethenians are alien in the same way people we "know" are alien: not so much in using different *rules* for putting meaning together (interpreting their irony and indirection is not different from interpreting our own), but in performing insincere speech acts or in denying the sincerity of the other's speech acts. In short, language is not the barrier, but the barrier can manifest itself in language. To be sure, the speech-act explanation of her technique does seem to reduce the confrontation to a "mere" misunderstanding. That is not, I think, an unfortunate consequence of the critical method; rather, the method only points up in stronger relief this characteristic of her art: as she elevates the dilemma of confrontation with the "other" to imaginative interest, she also domesticates it.

The second task Le Guin accomplishes is the depiction of the gradual process of lowering the barriers. She does this in two ways: (1) by having the characters use freely certain kinds of direct speech acts that make them vulnerable to each other, and (2) by showing the characters' increased consciousness about the significance they attach to certain speech acts.

Confessions of fault, avowals of belief, apologies — expressed in direct form — appear in greater proportion after Estraven rescues Genly Ai from near death in Pulefen Voluntary Farm. These seem to make the characters vulnerable to each other because their sincerity and essential conditions require, to some extent, that each of them enter into the intentions of the other. Their speech acts contain reports on each character's state of mind. Of course, as noted before, we cannot make an equation between certain kinds of speech acts and certain values, but a change in the proportion of certain speech acts gives the impression that a new relationship is being negotiated between the parties. Though there are such things as "insincere" promises, apologies, and the like, a change in their proportion to assertions and questions, the usual mode of communication, could be used to express a change in the relationship between speaker and hearer. In *LHD* these direct speech acts manifest a series of upwellings from Genly Ai's subconscious as the truths he has suppressed make their way toward the surface and as Estraven attempts to channel those upwellings. In a sense, Estraven's rescue has given Genly, in an unmistakable way, all that he needs to know to credit everything Estraven tells him; and what he tells him — about Lord Tibe's machinations against the Envoy, about his own efforts to protect Genly Ai — provides the pattern in which the rescue is only the final piece. The rescue acts as voucher not only for Estraven's earlier attempt to give (indirect) advice, but for the subsequent (direct) speech acts as well. In the confrontation after Pulefen, we see Genly Ai painfully attempting to fit the new information into his mode of understanding Estraven's speech acts.

Genly asks his usual clarification-questions, and Estraven answers them, with less attempt at wit and charm than characterized his conversation in Ehrenrang. But at the end of each pulse of questions and answers (themselves for the most part direct speech acts) comes a direct speech act in which the impact of Estraven's information registers upon Genly Ai. The first registering is Genly's exclamation of "frustration": "All right . . . I see, I believe you." Clearly, the frustration arises because the rescue that Estraven describes would undermine Genly's edifice of distrust. Thus he grants the confession of belief only to the act itself, attempting to reserve the meaning such an act implies. "But I don't understand. I don't understand what you did all this for" begins the next pulse of questions and answers. Estraven controls his anger and explains that he had to protect Genly from the machinations of Tibe, whose ascension to power prevented Genly's mission from success in Karhide and made Orgoreyn his next logical step for Genly. Still, Genly asks, and the Tibean subtext is evident, "What were you after?" When Estraven explains that his goal was the same as Genly's, Genly blurts out, "How the devil can I believe anything you say!" Genly perhaps senses that this exclamation, taken as a question, is readily answered by the fact of the rescue, and it is the pain of giving up his own cherished pattern of interpretation that causes this outburst.

Estraven then initiates a new tack: if he can give up his cultural biases to some extent, he can perhaps bring down the barrier which prevents Genly from acknowledging his sincerity. Estraven's response is a direct speech act. Though "not used to giving or accepting advice or blame," he accepts fault and failure, completing the assertion begun by Genly: "Your efforts on my behalf — Have failed. And have put you in pain, and shame, and danger." In return, he makes Genly accept blame as well: "I am the only man in all Gethen that has trusted you entirely, and I am the only man in Gethen that you have refused to trust." Genly's apology is in a manner a verification of Estraven's assertion, as Estraven's was a completion of Genly's. The reciprocity signals the beginning of that development of "we-feeling" which will lead to love and, in an unexpected manner, the fulfillment of the charge of the Ekumen.

Throughout the rest of the novel we see an increasing number of "confrontations" and victories by means of direct speech acts. Although I do not have space to analyze them all, I can at least mention the increased freedom with which Estraven gives orders and admits fault, and the fact that, eventually and reluctantly, he gives direct advice. These would suggest that Estraven has transcended the customs of his culture to a significant extent. Genly Ai's transcendence is evident in a change in his own speech acts as well as in his increased consciousness about the significance he attaches to certain kinds of speech acts and in his gradual revision of this significance.

In the scene following Genly's unhappy apology, we see evidence that he has begun to accept Estraven's cultural bias against direct advice-giving. Estraven's answers to Genly's probings about the proposed trek across the Gobrin Ice are direct, but he gives only information; he does not say "we should" or "I advise," and Genly still transacts his part of the conversation by direct questioning ("Where do we go from here?"), as usual treating what he clearly sees as advice as if it had been directly proposed ("All right"). The main difference in Genly's questions is that they no longer carry an indirect accusation, but seem only to elicit what Estraven is thinking. Genly cooperates with Estraven in this conversation as if in a joint effort to bring all information into the open so that the right action may be taken; he does not force Estraven to give advice directly.

With his increase of trust, Genly seems to have relinquished a little of his need for explicitness. This seems of a piece with his increased respect for the communicative power of silence, a theme which gains richness from this point on in the novel as Genly successively discovers Estraven's oneness with the silent and silencing landscape, admits Estraven's sexual wholeness, and allows Estraven his own secrecies, the personal reasons that make him resist mind-speech. Through these means, he comes to appreciate the potentially good reasons for the predominance of indirections in Gethenian speech: they are in a way like the silences which, in the view of Martin Buber, whom Le Guin consciously invokes in this novel, admit the integral existence of the "other." This heightened appreciation of the silences in speech culminates in the scene at the inn where the two finally take refuge. Genly listens to Estraven's conversation with the cook; Estraven conveys essential information while suppressing all details. The indirections in Estraven's communication now seem through Genly's eyes a part of Estraven's perfect solicitude for the safety of his hosts: not as evasion, but as a perfect respect for the "other." This depiction contrasts markedly with his reaction to Estraven's conversation with himself in Ehrenrang.

This resolution is reached gradually, however, and Le Guin marks each stage in Genly's understanding of the significance of speech acts.

The conversations after Pulefen suggest that Genly has accepted the necessary assumption of the speaker's sincere conscious intent to benefit the hearer and has allowed for the cultural restrictions of the other, but they have not yet touched the sexual barrier which still prevents the full flowering of the "I-Thou" relationship. When, after a sleepless night, severe indigestion brought on by eating meat, and a strenuous haul across the ice, Genly Ai is ordered by Estraven to stop work and lie down, he takes offense at the directness of the speech act. In his culture only inferiors, children, and women are given direct orders. It is significant that in his silent rebellion, he recovers his role by characterizing himself as a stallion, Estraven as a (sterile — and sexless?) mule. He interprets the orders as Estraven's attempt to enhance his own masculinity at the expense of Genly's. The incipient altercation is laid to rest, however, when Estraven indicates that he thought Genly was still sick. Genly can accept *this* motivation for giving orders: "He, after all, had no standards of manliness, of virility, to complicate his pride. On the other hand, if he could lower all his standards of shifgrethor, as I realized he had done with me, perhaps I could dispense with the more competitive elements of my masculine self-respect, which he certainly understood as little as I understood shifgrethor." But Genly has not really penetrated to the sexual motives for his reaction. Here he is content to draw in his horns when he finds he has not been really threatened. He can do so the better by finding a similarity, at least of compulsion, between his masculine pride and Gethenian shifgrethor, in his eyes a virtually sexless concept.

In a still later scene, Estraven rebuffs his attempts at conversation (he is in kemmer and would avoid contact). Genly does not take offense but begs Estraven to explain what offense he has given against shifgrethor:

> We were both silent for a little, and then he looked at me with a direct, gentle gaze. His face in the reddish light was as soft, as vulnerable, as remote as the face of a woman who looks at you out of her thoughts and does not speak. And I saw then again, and for good, what I had always been afraid to see, and had pretended not to see in him: that he was a woman as well as a man. Any need to explain the sources of that fear vanished with the fear; what I was left with was, at last, acceptance of him as he was.

The difference in Genly Ai's reaction this time is immediately evident.

Instead of characterizing Estraven as a mule, he describes him in evocative terms as a desiring and desirable woman. What Genly discovers
here is a quite different being from the one he has been characterizing as
"the other" in his conversational transactions. The unconscious purposes
Genly had attributed to Estraven — that is, the attempt to enhance his
own masculinity at the expense of Genly's — had already been abandon-
ed. But behind this attribution of purpose, there lay in his earlier deal-
ings with Estraven an unconscious fear of Estraven as both feminine and
masculine, the fear of being seduced. Even in the scene in the Corner
Red Dwelling he had seen the feminine in Estraven — the charm, the
tact — which Genly had rejected as "his effeminate deviousness."

Why does Genly now not find this being even more threatening
than the masculine one? By gradations Genly had come to expect and
even desire the emergence of this being. His salvation at Estraven's
hands has stripped away the rationalization that attributes perfidy to
Estraven's femaleness. He has had to relinquish this concept of Estraven
as an aggressive male like himself and with similar needs to prove his
maleness. More than that, his aloneness with Estraven, who therefore
becomes his only image of humankind, makes Genly see Estraven as
neither male nor female and as both, as the whole counterpart to his
fragmented self. Though Le Guin has them reject sexual intercourse,
she does not have them reject the desire: Genly can see Estraven as a
potential lover and himself as beloved.

This realization does affect Genly Ai's characteristic handling of
speech acts. For one thing, he can (in terms of his own culture) accept a
"female" speech behavior for himself. In a later scene, when Genly Ai is
driven to an access of tension by the terrors of crossing the crevassed ice,
he stops in his tracks, unable to go further, tears freezing on his lids.
This time he says simply, "I'm afraid"; and when Estraven orders him to
make camp, he protests only feebly. More importantly, he now posses-
ses the key to a better appreciation of Gethenian speech acts, a recognition of "the other" as a whole person, not simply as a flawed version of
himself.

In Le Guin's technique, the speech act *can* hide information. But it
can also be used to communicate; and, communicating more than its
literal content, it can be the means of wit and play, the means of conveying respect. Le Guin, grasping the complex structure of the speech act,
sees it as the evolved form of communication which extends "the complexity and intensity" of human life. Language, though it is apparently

antithetical to silence, has left room for the deeper silence that finds its way into speech by means of indirection.

Because speech-act theory can, as we have seen, take in certain extra-linguistic conditions, it can be adapted to describing the interactions which constitute a large part of the plot of *LHD*. There are limitations, of course. Though capable of pointing to the *necessity* of contextual information and of showing in a formal way by what avenues it is connected with language (the felicity conditions), speech-act theory does not indicate *why* a particular speaker may resort to such circumlocutions as indirect speech acts and figurative language in a particular context, or what particular connotative value a community may associate with a speech act. The theory does not tell why, for example, giving an order is seen in our culture as an insult, if given by one man to another his supposed equal in age, position, and talents. Moreover, although it makes room for personal experiences and interpretations in so far as it provides an avenue for the mental contents of speaker and hearer to bear on the speech act, it does not show exactly *how* these experiences and interpretations aid or subvert communication. Its only task is a general description of the possibility of communication, whereas it is the task of the linguist proper or of the reader/critic to explain the dynamics of the particular verbal transaction. Speech-act theory defines the preparatory and sincerity conditions as the points in conversation vulnerable to breakdown. The reader/critic can show how the SF writer sensitive to the workings of communication focuses on these points and creates the psychological and anthropological information that constitutes the interpretative context for the character's conversations. As a result, the native language of the reader becomes the instrument of alienation and familiarization and shows the alienness and familiarity of his or her own culture.

Optimism and the Limits
of Subversion in *The Dispossessed*
and *The Left Hand of Darkness*

Carol McGuirk

> *He hunted through an overflowing drawer and finally achieved a book, a queer-*
> *looking book, bound in blue. . . . The title was stamped in gold and seemed to say*
> Poilea Afio-ite, *which didn't make any sense, and the shapes of some of the letters*
> *were unfamiliar. Shevek stared at it, took it from Sabul, but did not open it. He*
> *was holding it, the thing he had wanted to see, the alien artifact, the message from*
> *another world.*

> (*The Dispossessed*)

Le Guin coolly subverts "pulp" exoticism: it is a prosaic (though queer-looking) textbook and not the star-washed ship viewscreen of space opera that offers young Shevek his first glimpse of a wider cosmos. Yet the passage also suggests the limits that Le Guin places on her portrayal of the alien—the "other"—in her two finest science fiction novels. Shevek's "alien artifact" is, in fact, from no alien world: it is a text in his own field, physics, by a scientist of Urras, the planet from which Shevek's own ancestors migrated some 170 years before the events described in *The Dispossessed*.

The people of Urras are of the same stock as the people of Anarres: the two worlds are not so much alien as estranged. Representing not the unknown but the previously known and rejected, Urras is to Shevek's people a rejected mother-world: the formidable solidarity of the Anarresti

---

From *Modern Critical Views: Ursula Le Guin,* edited by Harold Bloom.©1985 by Carol McGuirk. Chelsea House Publishers, 1985.

originated in their shared hatred of Urrasti oppression. (Similarly, on the level of characterization, Shevek himself is shown as having matured through his conscious rejection of Rulag, his own nonnurturing mother.)

Repeatedly in the "Hainish" novels, the apparent alien becomes, on better acquaintance, really a repressed, rejected, or earlier phase of the self. When the Earth envoy Genly Ai reaches his Gethenian friend Therem Harth telepathically, it is the voice of his dead brother that the terrified Lord of Estre "hears." An analogous paradox structures Freud's analysis of the uncanny: the world *"heimlich,"* he notes, grades easily into its opposite: *unheimlich,* not homelike, terrifying. Le Guin's vision of the alien works in a more optimistic direction, seeing beyond apparent "otherness" to a connectedness — she sometimes calls it "human solidarity" — that goes beneath and beyond apparent difference. This model is, as Le Guin has noted, Jungian and romantic (the collective unconscious is the source of individual identity) rather than Freudian and ironic. (To Freud, such "oceanic" certainties are simply memories of one's deluded sense of omnipotence in infancy.)

The first level of optimism in Le Guin, then — and the primary reason for her suppression of the alien — is psychological. In *The Left Hand of Darkness,* the Gethenians are, like the people of Anarres and Urras and indeed like the Earth envoy Genly Ai, all of common ancestry. Earth, like Gethen — and like the Cetian solar system described in *The Dispossessed* — was seeded with sentient life by the proto-human colonizers called the Hainish. In Le Guin's cosmos, as in Cordwainer Smith's, there is no true "other" — all intelligent life has a common origin and a common humanity. All advanced species have the capacity for "mindspeech," or telepathy — science fiction's most powerful image of communion. Since the human psyche is notably flawed, planetary cultures may well evolve in troubling ways: social injustice is a central concern in Le Guin's fiction. Yet the final message always seems to involve the ultimate bridgeability of difference — at least by characters of heroic capacity. Le Guin's heroes are strong enough to resist the pressures of xenophobia (the hatred of apparent difference), and wise enough to take as their goal the greater good of humanity; this often requires the "betrayal" of some smaller group. One such character is Shevek, the exile/traitor/hero of *The Dispossessed:* "I want solidarity, human solidarity. I want free exchange between Urras and Anarres." Another is Therem Harth of Estraven, the exile/traitor/hero of *The Left Hand of Darkness:* "Do you think I would play *shifgrethor* when so much is at stake for all of us, all my fellow men? What does it matter which country wakens first, so long as we waken?"

Such heroes are not pasteboard saints: they are self-willed individuals whose magnanimous loyalties lead them past temptation and well into transgression. In his youth, Therem Harth breaks the incest taboos of his planet by vowing *kemmering* (marriage) with his brother; later, he breaks other social codes when he steals and, perhaps, when he chooses to die. Shevek, too, despite his fierce love for Anarres, is often, because of his genius, incapable of satisfying its egalitarian prinicples. At two, he is reprimanded for claiming that the sun belongs to him; at eight, he is punished for "egoizing" in his study group. At forty, he will donate his scientific breakthrough, the theory of simultaneity, to the Hainish, in order to prevent it from being put to partisan uses. Such heroes are intuitive, and their intuitions are vindicated. Their allegiance to an idealized human community protects them from misanthropy, yet their clear-sighted openness to the "message from another world" comes from their habitual sense of distance from their native groups — another of Le Guin's paradoxes. Genly Ai says of Therem Harth: "He was always ready. It was, no doubt, the secret of the extraordinary political career he threw away for my sake; it was also the explanation of his belief in me and devotion to my mission. When I came, he was ready. Nobody else on Winter was."

Le Guin's conception of heroism, then, is — like the ubiquity of human values in her cosmos — admirably enlightened yet somehow also fundamentally optimistic, denying the ineluctable difference of the truly alien by making the central feature in heroic behavior a refusal to *be* alien-ated. Le Guin's heroes insist on the negotiable status of difference; the plots of both of *The Dispossessed* and *The Left Hand of Darkness* involve successful negotiation. Le Guin's Hainish cosmos is thus tailored to demonstrate the power of individual heroes, the altruism of their heroic impulse, the advancement of society through violation of its laws, and the persistence of humane values despite often unfavorable cultural conditions. (Genly Ai, imprisoned in totalitarian Orgoreyn and moved by the special treatment given him by fellow-prisoners, muses: "It is a terrible thing, this kindness that human beings do not lose.")

Above all, Le Guin's cosmos is ethical, designed to provide a setting for the drama of human choice. Fredric Jameson has called her procedure "world-reduction," but it also involves an inflation of individual human agents. Shevek's renegade physics research — the transgression of one man — leads to the theory of simultaneity. The Ekumen establishes contact with newly discovered worlds by sending a single Envoy:

"The first news from the Ekumen on any world is spoken by one voice, one man present in the flesh, present and alone." Isolation is power: as Therem Harth warns Obsle of Orgoreyn, the unarmed defenseless Envoy "brings the end of Kingdoms and Commensalities with him in his empty hands." This Hainish cosmos is a vigorously enabling one—and it consistently rewards those heroes and cultures that tolerate diversity. It is Cetian physics that penetrates the mysteries of space and time, because Cetian science—unlike that of hapless "Ainsetain of Terra," a genius trapped in a less enabling world—has always encouraged eclecticism:

> The Terrans had been intellectual imperialists, jealous wall-builders. Even Ainsetain, the originator of the [relativity] theory, had felt compelled to give warning that his physics embraced no mode but the physical and should not be taken as implying the metaphysical, the philosophical, or the ethical.
>
> (*The Dispossessed*)

By contrast, in Le Guin's refreshingly anti-imperialist cosmos, "the strongest, in the existence of any social species, are those who are most social. In human terms, most ethical." This is fundamentally a Renaissance or humanist cosmology—the Universe, like the text, is constructed to incarnate Man ("one man present in the flesh"). Humanity is the subject and the object of all texts and all messages: the ansible, like the radios of Karhide and like "mindspeech," transmits a single human voice.

Scholars who approach Le Guin through the field of utopia/eutopia/dystopia—a flourishing academic specialty in recent years—find her idealized, humanized cosmos less problematic than some other factions in science-fiction studies (one might term the dissidents "hard science" fundamentalists or cosmological gnostics). Such critics are prone to fears that utopia is not now the avant-garde literary form that it was in 1516, and that—however enlightened humanism's original secularization of value—the Renaissance emphasis on the reasonableness of human nature and the intelligibility of the cosmos detracts from some of the more powerfully subversive symbolic possibilities of the science fiction genre.

The eloquent if splenetic Stanislaw Lem has summed up this viewpoint succinctly in a general indictment of American SF's tendency to "domesticate" the cosmos. In his view, which is taken from the standpoint of contemporary cosmology, "it makes no sense at all to look at the universe from the viewpoint of ethics":

The universe is a continued explosion extended over a time of twenty billion years [that] could appear as a majestic solidification only to the eyes of a transient being like man. . . . Thanks to time travel and FTL [faster-than-light spaceships], the cosmos [of American SF] has acquired such qualities as domesticate it in an exemplary way for storytelling purposes; but at the same time it has lost its strange, icy sovereignty. . . . The fact that a domestication of the cosmos had taken place, a dimunition that [has] whisked away those eternally silent abysses of which Pascal spoke with horror, is masked in SF by the blood that is so liberally split in its pages. But there we already have humanized cruelty, for it is a cruelty that can be understood by man, and a cruelty that could finally even be judged from the viewpoint of ethics. . . . We [thus] come to understand what SF has done to the cosmos: for it makes no sense at all to look at the universe from the viewpoint of ethics. Therefore the universe of SF is not only miniscule, simplified and lukewarm, but it has also been turned towards its inhabitants, and in this way it can be subjugated by them, losing thereby [its] indifference. . . . In the universe of SF there is not the slightest chance that genuine myths and theologies might arise, for the thing itself is a bastard of myths gone to the dogs. The SF of today is a "graveyard of gravity," in which that subgenre that promised the cosmos to mankind, dreams away its defeats in onanistic delusions and chimeras — onanistic because they are anthropocentric.

(*SF Studies* 4 [1977])

Although Lem's charge of excessive violence is hardly applicable to the consistently responsible and pacifist fiction of Le Guin, his attack on the "domestication" of the cosmos does suggest a troubling limitation in her vision — an optimism that too easily tames the universe by denying its perilous otherness. Thoroughly secular, admirably ethical, Le Guin's universe nonetheless achieves its balance and coherence through a diminished emphasis on the unknowable, the alien; the "silent abysses of which Pascal spoke with horror" are made, perhaps too readily, to speak to us here and now. This may be what David Ketterer means in *New Worlds for Old* when he criticizes *The Left Hand of Darkness* for the overt didacticism that he calls "insufficiently displaced myth." Lem's critique is broader: in general, American SF's pastoral parable of a hero-enabling, navigable cosmos indulge in downright misrepresentation of the physical universe — and thus fail to delineate our real dilemma:

> The space surrounding a neutron star cannot be passed close-ly in a spaceship even at parabolic velocity because the gravi-ty gradients in a human body increase . . . and human beings explode until only a red puddle is left, just like a heavenly body that is torn apart from tidal forces when pass-ing through the Roche limit.

Le Guin has said that she does "not like to see the word 'liberal' used as a smear word," and given the often reactionary leanings of popular SF (of which, more later) there is courage and risk in her liberal stance. Still, if Darko Suvin's definition of SF as "the literature of cognitive estrangement" is correct (as I think it is), there is also some evasiveness — some stopping short of radical re-visioning — in Le Guin's humane liberalism. Science fic-tion, with its potentially powerful imagery of voyages into the unknown and encounters with the alien, is probably better designed to subvert than to validate human-centered norms and values. (Indeed, Le Guin's an-drogynes in *The Left Hand of Darkness* are used, early in the novel, in such a subversive way. The Gethenians, with their lack of institutionalized sex-ism and gender anxiety, force readers to ponder their own preconceptions about gender and identity. Yet while strongly making that point — and, along the way, joyously puncturing a number of SF's most cherished sexist cliches — Le Guin finally imposes over her subversive surface, a human-ist/Taoist fable of oneness and reconciliation. There is a humanity beyond gender difference, evident in mindspeech, in the Gethenians' "human" pronoun, and in Genly Ai's final ability to understand and love Therem Harth. Subversion of traditional gender roles in this novel, then, ulti-mately serves the purpose of affirming a familiar progressive value: tolerance for diversity.)

Le Guin's liberalism, in short, while admirable in questioning ster-eotypes and rejecting the easy violence and repellent social Darwinism of so much popular SF, is nonetheless content to dwell on the knowable (indeed, heroic) capacities of human nature, never striking into the heart of true darkness: the morally problematic existence of intransigent evil, and the cosmologically problematic fact that our universe poses liter-ally unimaginable dangers. Lacking these dark intonations — or rather given her Jungian/Taoist value for darkness as a benign and necessary balance to light — Le Guin's human-centered, progressive vision can degenerate, as Samuel Delany has noted, into sentimentality. This is an occasional flaw in the portrayal of life on Anarres (e.g., "However pragmatic the morality a young Anarresti absorbed, yet life overflowed in him, demanding altruism, self-sacrifice, scope for the absolute gesture" — the implied definition of "life" here forces its idealism on readers). Sentimentality sometimes strikes a false note even from the scrupulously honest, plain-spoken, unforgettable narrators of *The Left Hand of Darkness:* "They were as sexless as steers. They were without shame and without desire, like the angels. But it is not human to be without shame and desire." The words are spoken by Genly Ai, but in their tacit assumption that humanity is the endpoint of creation they are worthy of *Star Trek's* constantly thwarted but incurably anthropocentric Dr. McCoy.

The real limit to subversion in Le Guin, then, is her tendency to an unexamined humanism: human capacities are given, rather too readily, a cosmic heroic stature. This is common among practitioners of "soft" SF, intent on replacing the technological emphasis of "hard" SF with a reemphasis on characterization. (It is also common among SF's libertarians, confident that institutions and laws are unnecessary restrictions on liberty, given the fundamental decency of individual human consciences.) Yet there are alternatives to an optimistic, utopian cosmology available in the popular science-fiction tradition. A brief discussion of Cordwainer Smith and Arthur C. Clarke — two writers who in different ways exploit SF's more radical possibilities — may help to place Le Guin's mediating liberalism. It will also introduce the final topic of this essay: Le Guin's ambivalent relationship to popular SF and her most consistently subversive activity — her energetic reversal of science fiction's common stock of tropes.

Cordwainer Smith was the pseudonym of Paul Linebarger (1913–66), a Johns Hopkins professor, foreign affairs consultant, and military intelligence expert (he coined the term "psychological warfare"). Le Guin dates her adult interest in SF from 1960, when she encountered "Alpha Ralpha Boulevard," her first Cordwainer Smith story: "I don't really remember what I thought when I read it, but what I think now I ought to have thought when I read it is, *"My God! It can be done!"* (*Foundation* 4 [1974]). Although ultimately the differences are more striking, there are many similarities between Le Guin and Smith. In Smith, as in Le Guin, all sentient life has a common source, although it is Terra, not Hain: the descendants of Earth colonists have settled the galaxy, and all intelligent life is Earth-derived. (There are intelligent animal species, genetically enhanced to serve as slaves to man, but the species are native to Earth. There are also true aliens, possibly from another galaxy—the elegant architects called the Daimoni—but they do not figure prominently in the stories.)

In Smith, as in Le Guin, the shared humanity of intelligent species is metaphorically underscored by universal latent telepathic abilities, called "hiering" and "spieking" in Smith. Le Guin, like Smith, sets her "Hainish" novels in different eras of a consistent future cosmos. (In a special Le Guin issue of *SF Studies* [1978], Rafail Nudelman praises the "originality" of her "future history drawn with a dotted line," but here Le Guin follows the practice not only of Cordwainer Smith but also of numerous other SF writers, from Asimov and Heinlein—who began the trend under the guidance of their editor during the 1940s, John W. Campbell—to H. Beam Piper and Frank Herbert.) Finally, like Le Guin, Smith is far more concerned with enduring human problems than with new technological solutions. In *Norstrilia,* the hero's trusty family retainer—a computer—answers Rod McBan's simple question "Who am I?" with a burst of eloquence:

> You are Rod McBan the hundred and fifty-first. Specifically, you are a spinal column with a small bone box at one end, the head, and with reproductive equipment at the other end. Inside the bone box you have a small portion of material which resembles stiff, bloody lard. With that you think—you think better than I do, even though I have more than five hundred million synaptic connections. You are a wonderful object, Rod McBan.

Cordwainer Smith's universe is thus, like Le Guin's, designed to explore and analyze the human psyche.

The difference is that Smith's analysis of the human dilemma is gloomier—his vision is religious rather than secular, fatalistic rather than optimistic and progressive. In Smith, unlike Le Guin, space is not easily navigable; monstrous adaptations are necessary to convey humans from planet to planet. In "The Game of Rat and Dragon," huge invisible "Rats" prey upon unprotected spacecraft; in *Norstrilia,* Rod McBan voyages to earth pickled and disassembled, packed in a crate the size of a hatbox. In "Scanners Live in Vain," set early in Smith's future history, something called the "Pain of Space" infects all early voyagers with a suicidal "need to die"—a problem that Smith solves fancifully by lining the walls of his ships with oysters, living tissue that absorbs the hostile cosmic vibrations and dies so that humans can retain their sanity.

(Animals who martyr themselves in the cause of man form a recurring theme in Smith; this may well be *his* area of sentimentality.)

Smith's pessimism is as consistently represented by his cosmos as Le Guin's progressive optimism by hers. In Smith, the rulers of Earth achieve eutopia only to find that humanity is on the decline: immortality, prosperity and peace have destroyed the suffering that Smith regards as essential to human identity. The rulers of the Instrumentality are forced to initiate the Rediscovery of Man, an emergency measure that reintroduces to earth the necessary human realities of war, disease, hatred and death. For all its emphasis on humanity, then, Smith's is a far less enabling cosmos than Le Guin's; in his postlapserian universe, human nature is to be redeemed through divine providence, not through social planning. In *Norstrilia,* the promise of redemption is represented by enslaved animals called the Underpeople, whose leader, the E'telekeli ("Entelechy," in Montaigne's paraphrase of Aristotle, is "the soul, or perfection moving of itself") is a fugitive, a failed genetic experiment—part eagle and part Daimoni. E'telekeli, father of E'kasus, is that quality, outcast from humanity and "other" than humanity (Daimoni are aliens), that nonetheless can redeem humanity. The politics are reactionary here (in that they suggest that the human condition is not improvable through political means), but the vision is radical in that evil is alive and awake in this universe. The reality of uncanny peril imbues the struggles of Smith's heroes with an authentic, if eccentric, intensity. What is subverted in Smith is precisely that eutopian dream of a perfectible—or at least reasonably nurturant— human community that is so strongly conveyed by Le Guin in such central images as the beneficent Ekumen. Ironically, Smith's religious conservatism leaves more room for mystery—for SF's exploration of "cognitive estrangement"—than Le Guin's more enlightened but less alienated humanist idealism.

Smith's is a High Church universe, hierarchical and paradoxical: the last shall be first. *Childhood's End,* Arthur C. Clarke's finest novel, offers a similar paradox couched in mystical rather than religious terms. Since Le Guin has been called a mystic because of her extensive use of paradox (a charge also frequently leveled at Jung), comparison of her work with *Childhood's End* may help to demonstrate the decidedly unmystical centrality of reason in her cosmos. In *Science Fiction: History, Form & Vision,* Scholes and Rabkin have called *Childhood's End* a utopian novel, but it is actually a parable about the limitations of enlightenment, indicated by the solely transitional value of the Golden Age achieved in its middle section. The real message combines a mystical quietism like that of Stapledon's

Star Maker (an influence Clarke acknowledges) with the child-as-monster theme beloved in pulp SF and best represented by Lewis Padgett's "Mimsy Were the Borogroves" and many of Ray Bradbury's early stories.

Clarke's consistent mysticism and Le Guin's preference for the rational are most clearly seen in their differing treatments of heroism and telepathy. In Clarke's novel, the exertions of the dare-all hero, Jan Rodricks, are poignant rather than effective. The cosmic rite of passage which humanity is about to undergo—the evolution and absorption of Earth's children into the pure energy entity call Overmind—makes Rodricks' venturesome individuality irrelevant. Nobody over the age of ten is recruited by Overmind: mature individuals are not of interest in this cosmos—they do not get very far. Seven-year-old Jeff Greggson travels further in his early dreams of the Overmind than the superior alien race, the Overlords, have travelled in their spaceships. Indeed, the ethical complexity and brilliant rationality of the Overlord's minds are exactly what makes them unsuitable for further evolution: they know that they will never progress into Overmind. In his conclusion, which Clarke says "repudiates optimism and pessimism alike," earth is destroyed by its departing children, yet the loss is a sign that humanity has evolved beyond the need for bodies, or an earth to contain them.

Clarke's Overmind—the most advanced cosmic entity—paradoxically seeks out immature beings to contact through telepathy. Children are not yet fully socialized; they have fewer barriers, less reliance on earthbound reasoning, than adults. In Le Guin, by contrast, telepathy is possible only in maturity. As Genly Ai tells Therem Harth: "Except in the case of the born Sensitive, the capacity (for mindspeech) . . . is a product of culture, a side-effect of the use of the mind. Young children, and defectives, and members of unevolved or regressed societies, can't mindspeak. The mind must exist on a certain plane of complexity first. . . . Abstract thought, varied social interaction, intricate cultural adjustments, esthetic and ethical perception, all of it has to reach a certain level before the connections can be made" (*LHD*). Far from embracing mysticism, then—if mysticism be defined as a yearning for self-loss and oneness—Le Guin, by contrast to Clarke, reveals a firm value for mature, rational individualism: in the Hainish novels, the libertarian in her is stronger than the Taoist. Yet, as with Smith's Christianity, Clarke's Buddhist mysticism may well leave more room for those powerful intonations of the unknown and the unknowable that SF is particularly well-suited to generating.

Perhaps the main point here is that utopia/eutopia/dystopia—the enlightened explorations, as in Le Guin, of exemplary societies—is, while clearly related to science fiction, just as clearly an older form, with closer ties to the optimistic assumptions of Renaissance humanism about human capacity. This optimism marks many passages in More's *Utopia:*

> [The citizens of Utopia] hold that happiness rests not in every kind of pleasure but only in good and decent pleasure. To such, as to the supreme good, our nature is drawn by virtue itself. . . . The Utopians define virtue as living according to nature. . . . [Reason] admonishes and urges us to lead a life as free from care and as full of joy as possible and, because of our natural fellowship, to help all other men, too, to attain that end.

In his emphasis on the innate rationality and altruism of human character, More sounds very much like Odo, founder of Anarres — a less ambiguous utopia than the subtitle of *The Dispossessed* would suggest.

Utopia, an inherently anthropocentric form, is not necessarily a genre that encourages its practitioners to use all the symbolic capacities of science fiction. While it may well explore social, sexual, and psychological "estrangement" (as Le Guin certainly does), it will seldom proceed to the cosmological estrangement explored by Clarke or the moral (as opposed to purely ethical) dilemmas posed by Smith. The utopian vision places the cosmos in the background in order to ensure that man remains in high relief; it deals with ethical rather than moral matters — with heroism rather than sin — because of a secular and classical focus inherited from Renaissance humanism. Perhaps another way to put this is to say that a utopia such as Anarres is political and thus dwells on the possible. Ideally, however, science fiction is equipped to range further, into the limits of the conceivable. Both Clarke and Smith, for instance, depict utopias solely to demonstrate their futility and to offer transcendent — if frightening — alternatives.

To emphasize the symbolic potential of science fiction in this way is not, incidentally, to suggest that scores of writers surpass Le Guin in their exploitation of the genre. Although Clarke and Smith do offer a more powerful representation of the cosmos, neither is the literary craftsman that Le Guin is, or comes close to her skill in characterization. Le Guin's limitations are simply imposed by the optimism of the humanist ideology and its literary offspring, utopia. Yet a large but misguided group within science fiction studies is now trying to legitimize SF by hitching its raffish wagon to a star — the older and, academically speaking, infinitely more respectable genre of utopia — and has encouraged the critical community to praise (in Le Guin and in contemporary utopian fiction generally) the very anthropocentric tendencies that are really limitations on what SF can accomplish.

Carl Yoke, for example, writing in *Extrapolation,* betrays this anxiety about respectability in remarks that sever Le Guin completely from the popular American tradition: "Without question, Le Guin is a writer of the first rank. . . . And she is a writer who is read by people who do not consider themselves to be science-fiction fans, who, in fact, scoff at the term 'science fiction.' . . . In this respect, Le Guin has done much to legitimize the genre, and as a result she has achieved 'mainstream' stature, just as H. G. Wells, Aldous Huxley and George Orwell have" (Fall 1980). Similar statements are often made and seldom challenged, but they raise at least two problems. The first has already been discussed: a marginal literary form serves highly useful and potentially subversive purposes, especially in its symbolic capaciousness, its greater freedom and fluidity of imagery. Why then should SF aspire to the mainstream? Secondly — and this is a new issue — such statements actually belittle Le Guin's achievement, for the British dystopians were never out of the mainstream in quite the sense that Ursula Le Guin was in 1966, when her first Hainish novel, *Rocannon's World,* appeared with Avram Davidson's *The Kar-Chee Reign* as an Ace Doubles paperback. (The Ace Doubles series was the apotheosis of pulp — two novels published back to back, under one cover, to cut costs. Donald A. Wollheim was the editor, and some fine fiction appeared in this throwaway format: the second Hainish novel, *Planet of Exile,* appeared later in 1966 paired with Thomas Disch's mordant *Mankind Under the Leash.*)

Wells, Huxley, and Orwell may have had their struggles, but they never had to publish their novels in tandem, or to deal with the often conflicting constituencies of American commercial SF: editors demanding quick sales, critics demanding high quality, fans demanding pure entertainment and frequent personal appearances at conventions. Le Guin's career has been almost unique in its graceful accommodation of such pressures. *The Left Hand of Darkness* and *The Dispossessed* won both the fans' Hugo and the SF writers' Nebula awards for the years in which they appeared (1969 and 1974); Le Guin is the only author who has twice won both awards simultaneously, demonstrating that these novels satisfied the highest expectations both of avid amateurs and SF professionals. Le Guin, who now publishes in *Critical Inquiry* and the *New Yorker,* is perceived by critics as a belletristic writer, yet the appeal of her science fiction to her original fannish constituency has never faltered. Indeed, the continuing high popularity of *The Left Hand of Darkness* and

The Dispossessed among fans may well be founded in a more intelligent response to Le Guin than her current critical modishness, which depends heavily on the unexamined assumption that utopia is, after all, an irreproachable intellectual enterprise. The fans, on the other hand, love Le Guin because of her provocative rendition of SF's themes and tropes—her witty reversals and re-visions of the pulp conventions in which fans are learned. The Handdara religion of Karhide says that "to oppose something is to maintain it," and Le Guin's revisions of the pulp tradition echo this paradox, both challenging and revivifying science fiction's characteristic narrative strategies.

A perspective by incongruity is afforded by Stanislaw Lem, who much resembles Le Guin in the use of reversal, paradox, and strategic understatement, but who is hostile rather than ambivalent toward the SF tradition. Lem's method, like Le Guin's, consists in an ascetic refusal of exoticism. Readers are re-educated and, upon any sudden irruption into the story, will see a cliche *as* a cliche. As a replacement for the standard space-opera sentence "The vast, unexplored planet loomed suddenly on the viewscreen," for instance, Lem offers us this:

> On day 1,006, having left the local system of the Nereid Nebula, I noticed a spot on the screen and tried rubbing it off with a chamois cloth. There was nothing else to do, so I spent four hours rubbing before I realized that the spot was a planet and rapidly growing larger.
>
> *(Memoirs of a Space Traveler)*

Retaliating against the mad-computer theme in popular SF (perhaps best exemplified by HAL in Kubrick and Clarke's *2001: A Space Odyssey*), Lem offers fables of sadomasochistic washing machines; and, in *Star Diaries,* of a planet supposedly colonized by a renegade computer but actually inhabited by humans in robot suits, accessories in an insurance scam. Musing on "the fundamental decency of the electronic brain," Lem's voyager Ijon Tichy concludes: "Only Man can be a bastard."

Le Guin's satire is aimed more at exhausted literary conventions than at human nature, but she uses the same tool: subversion of the SF reader's conditioned expectations. Using the SF scenario of the hero seeking refuge among benevolent aliens, for instance, Le Guin offers in *The Dispossessed* Shevek's encounter with *his* first alien—an employee of the Terran embassy on Urras:

"Shevek. My name is Shevek. From Anarres." The alien eyes

flashed, brilliant, intelligent, in the jet-black face. *"Mai-god!"* the Terran said under his breath, and then, in Iotic, "Are you seeking asylum?"

On Urras, Iotic is standard and English the "alien" tongue. *The Left Hand of Darkness* similarly reverses space-opera's view of the alien either as a threat to be subdued or a resource to be exploited. It is the Earth-born Genly Ai who is the alien intruder on Gethen, but he comes bearing no arms—just a message from the Ekumen, a clearing house of information about other worlds. Ai's outnumbered status is used to effective ironic purposes: his (in human terms) perfectly ordinary male gender is viewed by Gethenian consensus as a distasteful perversion. Yet, in a further reversal and denial of the exotic, Genly Ai looks so much like a Gethenian (albeit a sexually anomalous one) that he cannot persuade the bureaucrats of Orgoreyn that he *is* from outer space. Therem Harth admits that there are few external tokens of Genly Ai's difference: "[The Orgota] see him no doubt much as I first saw him: an unusually tall, husky and dark youth just entering *kemmer*. I studied the physicians' reports on him last year. His differences from us are profound. They are not superficial. [Yet] one must know him to know him alien." Bug-eyed monsters have not been fashionable in SF for decades, but a tendency to exteriorize "otherness" persists—and Le Guin's characterizations of the alien constitute a penetrating criticism of that tendency.

Le Guin's not-so-alien aliens may have their cosmological limitations, as mentioned earlier, but they very effectively challenge the often facile exoticism of popular SF. In conventional usage, the trope of the alien suggests that evil can be embodied somewhere beyond the human norm, and this evil bears an instantly recognizable and hateful shape. A memorable example occurs in Fredric Brown's "Arena," published in 1944 (the pulps became decidedly xenophobic during World War II, and this "red sphere of horror" suggests the central image on the Japanese flag):

And he was alone, but not alone. For as Carson looked up, he saw that red thing, the red sphere of horror which he now knew was the Outsider, was rolling towards him.

Rolling.

It seemed to have no legs or arms that he could see, no features. It rolled across the blue sand with the fluid quickness of a drop of mercury. And before it, in some manner he could not understand, came a paralyzing wave of nauseating, retching, horrid hatred.

(*SF Hall of Fame,* VOL. 1, P. 287)

In tacit response to this SF theme of alien-as-menace, Le Guin describes the country folk of Karhide in *The Left Hand of Darkness,* who welcome Genly Ai calmly and without curiosity: "An enemy is not a stranger, an invader. [In Karhide] the stranger who comes unknown is a guest. Your enemy is your neighbor." Thus, in Le Guin, evil is political, not racial: it is embodied in the secret police of Orgoreyn and Urras; in all-too-familiar, not in strange-looking shapes.

Social Darwinism — the notion that in society as in nature, only the fit survive — is often rendered in popular SF as a rationale to support competitiveness, aggression, and imperialism. This theme, like that of the exteriorized alien, is analyzed and disposed of in Le Guin's science fiction. The Hainish universe is a sadder but wiser place in which the adaptive purposes of aggression have been demonstrated to be nil. The Earth ambassador to Urras tells Shevek:

My world, my Earth, is a ruin. A planet spoiled by the human species. We multiplied and gobbled and fought until there was nothing left. We controlled neither appetite nor violence; we did not adapt. We destroyed ourselves. But we destroyed the world first. . . . You Odonians chose a desert; we Terrans made a desert. . . . We survive there, as you do. People are tough! There are nearly half a billion of us now. Once there were nine billion. You can see the old cities still everywhere. The bones and bricks go to dust, but the little pieces of plastic never do — they never adapt either. We failed as a species, a social species. We are here only because of the charity of the Hainish.

When Fredric Jameson calls *The Left Hand of Darkness* an "anti-*Dune,*" he suggests Le Guin's revisionary relationship to popular SF. Indeed, although both Herbert and Le Guin are libertarians, Le Guin precisely reverses the notion prevalent in the *Dune* series (and widespread in SF) that personal identity is achieved primarily in the struggle to subjugate or be subjugated — that all life is a holy war or Jihad. By contrast, the persecuted Odonian community on Urras is said to be striking, not for better wages, but "against power." And in

"American SF and The Other," Le Guin strongly expresses in critical terms the stance of her Hainish fiction, which consistently rejects popular SF's aggrandizement of power as a route to personal identity:

> If you deny any affinity with another person or kind of person, if you declare it to be wholly different from yourself — as men have done to women and class has done to class, and nation has done to nation — you may hate it, or deify it; but in either case . . . you have made it into a thing, to which the only possible relationship is a power relationship. And thus you have fatally impoverished your own reality. You have, in fact, alienated yourself.
>
> This tendency has been remarkably strong in American SF. The only social change presented by most SF has been toward authoritarianism, the domination of ignorant masses by a powerful elite — sometimes presented as a warning but often quite complacently. . . . Military virtues are taken as ethical ones. Wealth is assumed to be a righteous goal and a personal virtue. Competitive free-enterprise capitalism is the economic destiny of the entire Galaxy. In general, American SF has assumed a permanent hierarchy of superiors and inferiors, with rich, ambitious, aggressive males at the top, then a great gap, and then at the bottom the poor, the uneducated, the faceless masses, and all the women. The whole picture is, if I may say so, curiously "un-American." It is a perfect baboon patriarchy, with the Alpha Male on top, being respectfully groomed, from time to time, by his inferiors.
>
> Is this speculation? Is this imagination? Is this extrapolation? I call it brainless regressivism.
>
> (*The Language of the Night*)

It is appropriate that discussion of the inventor of Anarres and Odo should finally come full circle. Le Guin's most consistently subversive activity lies in her polemical reversals, in her ironic rendition of the popular SF tradition. Yet the source of her popularity and of her narrative power, as well as of her ideological limitations, lies in her calm but persistent placement of the human individual — never at war but always at risk — in the live center of her cosmos. The physics of Le Guin's Hainish cosmos are thus really metaphysics, although such scientists as Fritjof Capra would certainly endorse them:

Most of today's physicists do not seem to realize the philosophical, cultural and spiritual implications of their theories.
Many of them actively support a society which is still based
on the mechanistic, fragmented world view, without seeing
that science points beyond such a view, towards a oneness of
the universe which includes not only our natural environment but also our fellow human beings.

(The Tao of Physics)

Le Guin's metaphysics stress harmony rather than Capra's "unity"—a
resonance of disparate but cooperative parts rather than an immolation
of identity. (This is strongly imaged in *The Left Hand of Darkness* in her
description of Foretelling—a communal activity that utilizes abnormal
energies, making an orchestration of aberrations necessary to producing
valid prophecy.) In *Devotions,* John Donne wrote that: "Man consists of
more pieces, more parts, than the world. . . . And if those parts were
extended, and stretched out in man as they are in the world, man would
be the giant and the world the dwarf; the world but the map and man the
world." Le Guin's rendition of human presence in the cosmos employs
an analogous paradox, reversing the usual SF positionings of micro and
macrocosm.

Le Guin once jokingly wondered why no researcher had yet pro-
spected among the archives at Radcliffe and Columbia for nuggets from
her early academic work. While researching this essay at Columbia's
Butler Library, I did look up her master's thesis, "Aspects of Death in
Ronsard's Poetry"; in fact, it suggested the focus of this discussion.
Perhaps Le Guin's defense of Ronsard's optimism stands as the best re-
joinder to any emphasis here on limitations:

To say Ronsard saw life as good . . . is not to make of him a
kind of Pollyanna of the Renaissance. Scholars are sometimes condescending, perhaps, in their opinion of Renaissance optimism. Ronsard was as aware as any Platonist of
his time that there seems to be a fundamental flaw
somewhere, that perfection does not exist and happiness does
not last, in this world.

Ronsard's optimism, like that of the Hainish series Le Guin would conceive ten years after writing her thesis, is firmly founded in a value for
reason. Ronsard "moved on classical ground . . . and if he saw the
grave as dark, it was with the unmysterious darkness of earthly night."

Both in their humanism, which is also a demystification of superstition and regressivism, and in their harmonious, "unmysterious" rendering of darkness, the Hainish novels do suggest Le Guin's continuing and in some ways problematic value for an enlightened Renaissance optimism.

Chronology

1929	Born October 21 in Berkeley, California, to Theodora Kroeber, the author of *Ishi in Two Worlds,* and Alfred L. Kroeber, a noted anthropologist.
1947–51	Radcliffe College.
1951–53	Graduate work in French at Columbia University.
1953	Marries Charles Le Guin in Paris, on December 22.
1957	Birth of daughter Elizabeth in Moscow, Idaho.
1959	Birth of daughter Caroline in Portland, Oregon, subsequently the residence of the family.
1960	Death of Alfred L. Kroeber.
1964	Birth of son Theodore, in Portland.
1966	*Rocannon's World; Planet of Exile.*
1967	*City of Illusions.*
1968	*A Wizard of Earthsea.*
1969	*The Left Hand of Darkness.*
1971	*The Lathe of Heaven; The Tombs of Atuan.*
1972	*The Farthest Shore; The Word for World is Forest.*
1974	*The Dispossessed.*
1975	*Wild Angels; The Wind's Twelve Quarters.*
1976	*Very Far Away From Anywhere Else; Orsinian Tales.*
1978	*The Eye of the Heron.*
1979	*Malafrena; The Language of the Night.*
1980	*The Beginning Place.*
1981	*Hard Words.*
1982	*The Compass Rose.*
1985	*Always Coming Home.*

Contributors

HAROLD BLOOM, Sterling Professor of the Humanities at Yale University, is the author of *The Anxiety of Influence, Poetry and Repression,* and many other volumes of literary criticism. His forthcoming study, *Freud: Transference and Authority,* attempts a full-scale reading of all of Freud's major writings. A MacArthur Prize Fellow, he is general editor of five series of literary criticism published by Chelsea House. During 1987–88, he was appointed Charles Eliot Norton Professor of Poetry at Harvard University.

DAVID KETTERER teaches at Concordia University, Montreal. He is the author of *The Rationale of Deception in Poe* and *New Worlds for Old: The Apocalyptic Imagination, Science Fiction and American Literature.*

FREDRIC JAMESON is Professor of French and Humanities at Duke University. He is the author of *Marxism and Form, The Prison House of Language,* and *The Political Unconscious.*

DONALD F. THEALL is President of Trent University, Ontario.

MARTIN BICKMAN teaches English at the University of Colorado.

JEANNE MURRAY WALKER teaches at the University of Delaware at Newark and writes science fiction.

ERIC S. RABKIN is Professor of English at the University of Michigan. He is the author of *The Fantastic in Literature,* and has edited anthologies of science fiction.

BARBARA BROWN of Toronto is a teacher, writer, and editor.

VICTORIA MYERS is Associate Professor of English at Pepperdine University, where she teaches creative writing and linguistics.

CAROL MCGUIRK is Associate Professor of English at Florida Atlantic University. She is the author of *Robert Burns and the Sentimental Era* and is an editor of *Fantasy Review.*

Bibliography

Annas, Pamela J. "New Worlds, New Words: Androgyny in Feminist Science Fiction." *Science-Fiction Studies* 5, no. 2 (1978): 143–55.

Bittner, James W. *Approaches to the Fiction of Ursula K. Le Guin.* Ann Arbor: UMI Research Press, 1984.

Bloom, Harold, ed. *Modern Critical Views: Ursula K. Le Guin.* New York: Chelsea House, 1985

Bucknall, Barbara J. *Ursula K. Le Guin.* New York: Frederick Ungar, 1981.

Cogell, Elizabeth Cummins. *Ursula K. Le Guin: A Primary and Secondary Bibliography.* Boston: G. K. Hall, 1983.

De Bolt, Joe, ed. *Ursula K. Le Guin: Voyager to Inner Lands and to Outer Space.* Port Washington, N.Y.: Kennikat, 1979.

Huntington, John. "Public and Private Imperatives in Le Guin's SF." *Science-Fiction Studies* 2, no. 3 (1975): 210–21.

Lake, David J. "Le Guin's Twofold Vision: Contrary Image-Sets in *The Left Hand of Darkness.*" *Science-Fiction Studies* 8, no. 2 (1981): 156–64.

Moylan, Tom. "Beyond Negation: The Critical Utopias of Ursula K. Le Guin and Samuel R. Delany." *Extrapolation* 21, no. 3 (1980): 236–53.

Nudelman, Rafail. "An Approach to the Structure of Le Guin's SF." *Science-Fiction Studies* 2, no. 3 (1975): 210–21.

Olander, Joseph D., and Martin Harry Greenberg, eds. *Ursula K. Le Guin.* New York: Taplinger, 1979.

Porter, David L. "The Politics of Le Guin's Opus." *Science-Fiction Studies* 2, no. 3 (1975): 243–48.

Rhodes, Jewell Parker. "Ursula Le Guin's *The Left Hand of Darkness:* Androgyny and the Feminist Utopia." In *Women and Utopia: Critical Interpretations,* edited by Marleen Barr and Nicholas D. Smith, 108–20. Lanham, Md.: University Press of America, 1983.

Rosinsky, Natalie M. *Feminist Futures: Contemporary Women's Speculative Fiction.* Ann Arbor: UMI Research Press, 1984.

Scholes, Robert. *Structural Fabulation.* Notre Dame, Ind.: University of Notre Dame Press, 1975.

Slusser, George Edgar. *The Farthest Shores of Ursula K. Le Guin.* San Bernardino, Cal.: The Borgo Press, 1976.

Spivack, Charlotte. *Ursula K. Le Guin.* Boston: Twayne, 1984.
Suvin, Darko. "Parables of De-Alienation: Le Guin's Widdershins Dance." *Science-Fiction Studies* 2, no. 3 (1975): 265–74.
Theall, Donald F. "The Art of Social-Science Fiction: The Ambiguous Utopian Dialectics of Ursula K. Le Guin." *Science-Fiction Studies* 2, no. 3 (1975): 256–65.

Acknowledgments

"Ursula Le Guin's Archetypal 'Winter-Journey'" (originally entitled *"The Left Hand of Darkness:* Ursula K. Le Guin's Archetypal 'Winter-Journey'") by David Ketterer from *New Worlds for Old: The Apocalyptic Imagination, Science Fiction, and American Literature* by David Ketterer, © 1974 by David Ketterer. Reprinted by permission of the author and Doubleday & Company, Inc.

"World Reduction in Le Guin: The Emergence of Utopian Narrative" by Fredric Jameson from *Science-Fiction Studies* 2, no. 3 (November 1975), © 1975 by SFS Publications. Reprinted by permission.

"The Art of Social-Science Fiction: The Ambiguous Utopian Dialectics of Ursula K. Le Guin" by Donald F. Theall from *Science-Fiction Studies* 2, no. 3 (November 1975), © 1975 by SFS Publications. Reprinted by permission.

"Le Guin's *The Left Hand of Darkness:* Form and Content" by Martin Bickman from *Science-Fiction Studies* 4 no. 1 (March 1977), © 1977 by SFS Publications. Reprinted by permission.

"Myth, Exchange and History in *The Left Hand of Darkness*" by Jeanne Murray Walker from *Science-Fiction Studies* 6, no. 2 (July 1979), © 1979 by *SFS Publications.* Reprinted by permission.

"Determinism, Free Will, and Point of View in Le Guin's *The Left Hand of Darkness*" by Eric S. Rabkin from *Extrapolation* 20, no. 1 (Spring 1979), © 1979 by the Kent State University Press. Reprinted by permission.

"*The Left Hand of Darkness:* Androgyny, Future, Present, and Past" by Barbara Brown from *Science-Fiction Studies* 21, no. 3 (Fall 1980), © 1980 by the Kent State University Press. Reprinted by permission.

"Conversational Technique in Ursula Le Guin: A Speech-Act Analysis" by Victoria Myers from *Science-Fiction Studies* 10, no. 3 (November 1983), © 1983 by SFS Publications. Reprinted by permission.

"Optimism and the Limits of Subversion in *The Left Hand of Darkness*" (originally entitled "Optimism and the Limits of Subversion in *The Dispossessed* and *The Left Hand of Darkness*") by Carol McGuirk from *Modern Critical Views: Ursula Le Guin,* edited by Harold Bloom, © 1985 by Carol McGuirk. Reprinted by permission.

Index

Ai, Genly: acceptance of Estraven of, 43-44, 97-99, 113-14, 122; character of, 7, 12-13, 16-17, 41, 44, 76-77, 82, 97, 102, 106-7, 108-9; compared to Shevek, 41; conversation with Tibe of, 102-3, 105-6, 107, 109; as envoy from Ekumen, 7, 12, 14, 42, 76-77, 96-97, 103, 108, 118, 120, 130; and Estraven, 7, 9-10, 13, 16, 18-19, 20, 42, 55, 57-58, 59, 61, 71, 73, 78, 81, 84-86, 88, 90, 95, 97-98, 101, 103, 107-9, 110-14, 118; on Estraven, 57, 58, 98-99, 119; and free will, 85; on Gethen, 94; imprisonment of, 13, 16-17, 20, 73, 84, 110, 119; and problem of social communication with Estraven, 43; as narrator, 41, 54, 59, 71, 83-84; on Orgoreyn, 56; psychological perception of by Tibe, 103, 106
Alien language, invention of, 101, 102-3, 105-9, 110-11, 113-14
Aliens, in science fiction as the "other," 130-31
"Alpha Ralpha Boulevard" (Smith), 123
"Amazed," 5
Ambisexuality: psychosocial results on Gethen of, 8-10, 14-15, 29-31; as theme in *The Left Hand of Darkness,* 41

Analogy, as narrative technique in science fiction, 27
Anarres, relationship to Urras, 117-18
Androgyny: in Chinese mythology, 93; in creation myths, 91-93; definition of, 91-92; and gender, 92; in Genesis, 92; in human sexuality, 91-94; Jungian view of, 92; in Kabalistic literature, 93; Le Guin on, 91, 96, 99; in *The Left Hand of Darkness,* 92, 94, 122; in literature, 93-94; and monism vs. dualism, 8-9, 14-15, 91-92; in Shakespeare, 93; in *Siddhartha* (Hesse), 93-94
Androgyny (Singer), 91
Aphorisms: Estraven's use of, 82; use of in *The Left Hand of Darkness,* 81-82, 86
Apocalypse: as component of science fiction, 12; in *The Left Hand of Darkness,* 15, 16-17
Arek of Estre, and Therem of Stok, 61, 69, 70-71, 78, 81
"Arena" (Brown), the "other" in, 130-31
Argaven (king of Karhide), 13, 15, 59, 80, 83, 97
"Aspects of Death in Ronsard's Poetry" (Le Guin's master's thesis), 133
Austin, J. L., speech-act theories of,